Better
Than
Happiness

Better Than Happiness

GREG LAURIE

Better Than Happiness

Unless otherwise indicated, all scripture quotations are taken from the New King James Version.® Copyright © 1982 by Thomas Nelson, Inc. Used by permission. All rights reserved.

Scripture quotations marked NLT are taken from the Holy Bible, New Living Translation, copyright © 1996. Used by permission of Tyndale House Publishers, Inc., Carol Stream, Illinois 60188. All rights reserved.

Scripture quotations marked NIV are taken from the HOLY BIBLE, NEW INTERNATIONAL VERSION (North American Edition). Copyright © 1973, 1978, 1984 by International Bible Society. Used by permission of Zondervan Publishing House. All rights reserved.

Scripture quotations marked AMP are taken from the The Amplified Bible, Old Testament copyright © 1965, 1987 by the Zondervan Corporation. New Testament copyright © 1958, 1987 by The Lockman Foundation. Used by permission.

Scripture quotations marked TLB are taken from The Living Bible copyright © 1971. Used by permission of Tyndale House Publishers, Inc., Carol Stream, Illinois 60188. All rights reserved.

Scripture quotations marked KJV are taken from the Holy Bible, King James Version.

ISBN: 978-0-9777103-9-3
Published by: Allen David Publishers—Dana Point, California
Coordination: FM Management, Ltd.
Editor: Karla Pedrow
Cover design: Chris Laurie
Interior design: Highgate Cross+Cathey
Production: Highgate Cross+Cathey
Printed in the United States of America

Contents

"For it is God who works in you both to will and to do for His good pleasure."

Philippians 2:13

Preface

When Paul wrote his epistle to the believers at Philippi, he was not living in an ivory tower somewhere. He had been imprisoned in Rome for his faithful proclamation of the gospel. Chained to a Roman guard, he was living in a place of extreme discomfort, to say the least. For a guy like Paul, this was a very difficult fate to endure. Paul was a go-getter. He was doer. He was the kind of guy who would take the bull by the horns and get the job done. So for him to be immobilized, to be stuck in one place where he could not move about freely would have been very frustrating. Yet Paul knew a lot about suffering. In 2 Corinthians 11, we are given a glimpse into the suffering he endured for the sake of the gospel:

> Five different times the Jewish leaders gave me thirty-nine lashes. Three times I was beaten with rods. Once I was stoned. Three times I was shipwrecked. Once I spent a whole night and a day adrift at sea. I have traveled on many long journeys. I have faced danger from rivers and from robbers. I have faced danger from my own people, the Jews, as well as from the Gentiles. I have faced danger in the cities, in the deserts, and on the seas. And I have faced danger from men who claim to be believers but are not. I have worked hard and long, enduring many sleepless nights. I have been hungry and thirsty and have often gone without food. I have shivered in the cold, without enough clothing to keep me warm. (vv. 24–27 NLT)

If you think you have problems, consider these words of Paul. They were not a plea for sympathy; they were simply a statement of fact. He was saying, "I know what it is like to experience hardship." Yet here in Philippians, one of the "prison epistles," Paul is writing to us about joy when he is in a situation where one would not normally be very happy. In fact, this is probably the most buoyant, joyful, and happy letters that Paul ever wrote. Not that happiness and joy is absent in his other writings. It just jumps out more in this one. In the four chapters of Philippians, Paul mentions joy, rejoicing, or gladness at least nineteen times.

What Paul spoke of is still available to us today. It wasn't reserved for first-century believers or a select few. As we study this remarkable epistle to the Philippians, we will discover how we can live so that our happiness no longer depends on what happens to us. Instead, we'll learn about something better than happiness—something that springs from a deep inner joy and can only be found in a relationship with Jesus Christ.

Greg Laurie

CHAPTER ONE

The Pursuit of Happiness

It has been more than two hundred years since the founding fathers of the United States signed that document at Independence Hall known as the Declaration of Independence. Without question, it is an amazing document—amazing for a number of reasons in that it says something I have never heard of in any other foundational document for any other country on the planet. You know the words: "We hold these truths to be self-evident, that all men are created equal, that they are endowed by their Creator with certain unalienable Rights, that among these are Life, Liberty and the pursuit of Happiness."

"The pursuit of Happiness … " That phrase really arrests my attention. Actually written into the Declaration of Independence is the statement that we as Americans have the right to pursue happiness. It's as though the founding fathers laid down the gauntlet way back in 1776: the pursuit of happiness is part of being an American.

A lot of time has passed since then. Americans live better than any other people on the planet. So why do we feel so bad when we have it so good? Why do more Americans go to psychologists and psychiatrists than those in other nations? Why is the teenage suicide rate higher in the United States than anywhere else on the plane? What is the problem?

An Endless Cycle

By and large, we can boil it down to this: we are seeking to be happy, but we are going about it in the wrong way. For many of us, our happiness is entirely contingent on good things happening. When things are going well, we are happy. When the career is going well, we are happy. When it is not going well, we are not happy. When we get a new toy (I am not just talking about kids here), we are happy. When something goes wrong, when a newer version comes out, or when your neighbor gets one that is a little bit nicer than ours, suddenly we are unhappy. This is a cycle of life of sorts, because no matter how much we accumulate or how much we accomplish, we are always going to come up a little bit short.

No matter how handsome or beautiful you are, you will never be as handsome or as beautiful as you want to be. If you've ever spent time around an incredibly beautiful or strikingly handsome person, you have probably heard them complain about how flawed they are.

Or maybe you've thought, *If I just had the perfect wardrobe, then I would look wonderful and I know I would be happy.* But clothes never will be fashionable enough. Just when you have completely revamped your wardrobe and you are totally on the cutting edge of style, an entirely new trend will come along. A noted fashion guru will declare that everything you have in your wardrobe is hopelessly lame and out-of-date.

It is no different when it comes to what we drive. Cars never will be fast enough. I am amazed at how fast people want their cars to be. "This thing only does 200 miles per hour," someone will say. Where exactly are they planning on driving the thing? But they want it faster. Why? Just so they can say it is faster than yours.

Or you might go down to the electronics store and get that new stereo system you've been wanting. The sales associate tells you, "You'll want to get this system, and it will cost this much. But if you put in some subwoofers, this baby is going to rock! It is going to be great!"

As you start to get your checkbook out, he continues. "Now, you need to have a video system to go with it. You can get this big TV, or you can get a rear-projection unit. We have the latest model out. It is 40 feet high. You mount it on the side of your house."

So you basically go into bankruptcy buying the 40-foot-high rear-projection unit and the killer stereo system. You have it all set up. You are happy. Then your neighbor tells you, "I just got HDTV!"

"Oh? What is that?" you ask.

"Haven't you heard about high-definition television? This rear-projection stuff is out."

It goes on and on. Houses never will be large enough or elaborate enough. Relationships never will be romantic enough or fulfilling enough. Life is never full enough. This is the way life goes. Our happiness ebbs and flows with the events that unfold in our lives.

This is why Solomon said, "The eye never has enough of seeing, nor the ear its fill of hearing" (Ecclesiastes 1:8 NIV). No matter what you see, you want to see more. No matter what you hear, you want to hear more. It is never enough.

A Different Approach

The answer is to avoid chasing after the kind of happiness that I have just described, because you are always going to come up empty.

The problem with that kind of happiness is that it overlooks one very important factor: God.

C. S. Lewis said, "God designed the human machine to run on Himself. He Himself is the fuel our spirits were designed to burn, or the food our spirits were designed to feed upon. There is no other. … God cannot give us happiness and peace apart from Himself, because it is not there. There is no such thing."[1]

God offers something better than happiness, at least the world's version of happiness. But it is the kind of happiness that can only be experienced by the child of God. It is called joy.

Joy is the theme of Philippians, probably the most buoyant, joyful, and happy letter that the apostle Paul ever wrote. It is not that happiness and joy is absent in his other writings. But these themes simply jump out more in this epistle. At least nineteen times in Philippians' four chapters, Paul mentions joy, rejoicing, or gladness.

Ironically, Paul is writing about joy when he is in a place where one normally would not be very happy: in prison. How could Paul be so positive, so jubilant, and so joyful in such adverse circumstances?

We find an important element running through this epistle that tells us how we can experience this joy. It is the word "mind." Paul uses "mind" ten times and "think" five times in Philippians. Add to these the word "remember," and we find that Paul makes a total of sixteen references to the mind. So we see that the secret of Christian joy is found in the way a believer thinks.

This doesn't mean you can wave a magic wand over your life and make your problems go away. You will have problems. You will have conflicts. You will have difficulties. You will have times when your health gives out.

So what are you going to do? If you want to be joyful, you will need to learn to look at things differently.

This is not to suggest that Paul is advocating mind over matter, positive thinking, or possibility thinking. He is teaching something more theologically sound than that. It is something very realistic and applicable. It is in the way we look at things. We are going to get into that more as we go deeper into the book. Essentially Paul is saying to us that if you want to live happily and joyfully and in harmony with other people, you need to apply the principles in this epistle.

The Place to Start

Paul begins by reminding us of the fact that we must come on God's terms. A lot of people want the benefits of the Christian life without giving anything on their part. They want to experience the blessings, but they don't want to meet the criteria. But it doesn't work that way.

The first few verses of Philippians are the door that we must walk through. And if we don't walk through this open doorway, then we are not going to experience the joy that is found inside.

There are some clear conditions to experience this joy. Let's start with verse 1: "Paul and Timothy, bondservants of Jesus Christ, to all the saints in Christ Jesus who are in Philippi, with the bishops and deacons."

It would be very easy to breeze casually over this verse and miss a foundational truth, not only for understanding and appreciating this book, but the rest of the New Testament as well. This is the opening statement about the life of joy: you must be one of the saints. If you want to be joyful, then you must be a saint. You don't have to live in

Philippi. You can be a saint in Los Angeles, a saint in Dallas, a saint in New York City, a saint in Jerusalem, a saint in Melbourne, or a saint in one of the most obscure places on earth.

You might think, *Well, that rules me out. I'm no saint.* But let's understand what the word means. In our modern usage, "saint" is a word we reserve only for the most holy people. We say things like, "Mother Teresa was a saint," or, "My sainted mother, God bless her … " We think of the people who do a lot of good deeds as being saints. They may be. Or they may not be. We have to consider what the word really means in biblical terms.

In the Bible, "saint" simply speaks of a true believer. It is a word that can be used interchangeably with "Christian." A literal definition of "saint" means "one who is set apart and consecrated for the purpose of God's service. If you have dedicated your life to following Jesus Christ, then you are a saint. I am a saint too. You don't have to call me Saint Gregory, but I am one.

We don't think of saints that way, however. We think saints are required to have done a certain number of miracles and go through a special process and be canonized. But that is not what the Bible teaches. The Bible teaches that if you are a true believer in Jesus Christ, then in the eyes of God, you are a saint.

Yet there are people today who want the blessings of the Christian life without giving anything in exchange for it. They want to be happy and, if possible, joyful, but they want it their way, on their own terms. They want to have the goodies, but they don't want any other part of it.

Paul was saying that you can't live that way. If you want to experience the promises of joy, then you must first be a saint, a true believer.

God promises you a deep-seated joy that can be with you no matter what you are going through. But that joy can only be found if you are a saint.

So how do you become a saint? First of all, you must admit that you are a sinner. You must come to God, be sorry for your sin, and be willing to turn from it and put your complete faith in Jesus Christ as your Savior and Lord. Then He will pardon you and forgive you of every sin you have ever committed. He will make you a saint, a true believer. Then you can start experiencing the promises of joy that Paul talks about.

Paul didn't say, "When things are going well, I am happy. When they are not going well, I am not happy." Rather, he said, "I have learned in whatever state I am, to be content" (Phil. 4:11). Paul's contentedness came not from what he had, but from whom he knew. That is where your contentedness will come from too.

Making Progress

We don't venture far into Paul's epistle before arriving at this wonderful promise: "Being confident of this very thing, that He who has begun a good work in you will complete it until the day of Jesus Christ" (Phil. 1:6). God always finishes what He begins. He never leaves something half-done like we do. With human beings, you find unfinished books, unfinished songs, and unfinished buildings. Why? Sometimes it is a lack of resources. Sometimes it is even a lack of desire. A number of reasons, or possibly excuses, could be cited.

I am the kind of person who starts projects around the house and often doesn't finish them. I get bored with them, especially if they are more difficult than I thought they would be. I wish I was Mr. Fix-It. I wish I was the kind of guy who could go down to the hardware store, buy the right tools, come back, and make anything work. But I am the antithesis of Mr. Fix-It. I want to be Mr. Fix-It in my heart, but I am not. As a result, I will get into a project that overwhelms me, and I will abandon it.

God is not that way. God does not start something and then lose interest. God doesn't say, "I am going to change Greg Laurie. I am going to mold him," and then come back later and say, "Oh, he is so boring! I'm moving on to something else." God will bring to completion that which He has begun in my life and yours. Hebrews 12:2 tells us that He is the author and the finisher of our faith. It was God who started the work, and it is God who will finish it.

We are seeking to be happy, but we are going about it in the wrong way.

Sometimes you may feel as though you are not going to make it. If you are resisting and not meeting the criteria of experiencing God's joy, that is one thing. But if you are a Christian and are ready and willing to move forward spiritually, then you will. You will cross that finish line.

In Philippians 2, Paul tells us, "Continue to work out your salvation with fear and trembling, for it is God who works in you to will and to act according to his good purpose" (vv. 12–13 NIV). Here we see a balance. God is the one who is working in you. God is the one who will bring it to completion.

So why does Paul tell us to work out our own salvation with fear and trembling? Because there is God's part and our part. "Work out" could be better translated, "carry it to the goal and fully complete your own salvation with self-distrust." In other words, we recognize that we don't have the ability to do this on our own. Yet at the same time, we want to apply these principles in our lives as we appropriate the power of God that He has made available to us. God wants to complete this work, but He is looking for our cooperation.

At the same time, we can become overly introspective, spiritual hypochondriacs. Hypochondriacs always think they are ill. They are always going in and getting check-ups, but sometimes they need to just kick back and not worry about every ache and pain. Some represent a problem and need to be checked, but many of those things just go away. Hypochondriacs can go overboard that way.

Just Be Patient

As Christians, we can overdo it and always be taking our spiritual temperature: *How am I doing spiritually today?* Five minutes later: *How am I doing spiritually right now?* We need to recognize that it takes time to be conformed into the image of Jesus.

It is like going on a new diet. At first, you wonder if you are losing any weight, so you end up weighing yourself every hour, noting every half-pound gain or loss. What you need to do is stick to your diet and then someone will come up to you one day and say the nicest thing a person could say, maybe other than "God bless you," which is, "Did you lose some weight?" Your new diet is working, but it takes time.

In Philippians 1:6, the words "has begun" and "complete" represent the bookends of life: "Being confident of this very thing, that He who *has begun* a good work in you will *complete* it until the day of Jesus Christ" (emphasis mine). From the original language, the word "complete" used here could be translated, "to perfect or finish." The One who has started this work in your life will finish it.

But when will this happen? When will you reach this state of perfection? I can tell you one thing: it won't take place this side of heaven. And anyone who tells you they have reached perfection is not only lying to you, but is also deluded.

The British preacher Charles Spurgeon, who was known for his eloquence and great sermons as well as his pranks and humor, was approached one day by two men who told him they had reached sinless perfection. As they were making their case, Spurgeon noticed a pitcher of very cold water sitting nearby. He picked it up and dumped it on both their heads. When the men reacted as any mere mortals would, he knew they had not reached the state they claimed to have reached.

If anyone could have reached a state of perfection, if anyone could have reached a spiritual plateau beyond all of us, it certainly would have been the apostle Paul. After all, Jesus called him on the Damascus Road. Under the inspiration of the Holy Spirit, he wrote a good portion of the Bible that we read today. He was caught up into the third heaven and saw things that he could not even describe. Yet Paul himself said, "Not that I have already attained, or am already perfected; but I press on, that I may lay hold of that for which Christ Jesus has also laid hold of me" (Philippians 3:12). Paul was essentially saying that we need to keep moving forward spiritually. We need to keep growing and learning. There is always so far to go.

If you are a follower of Jesus Christ, you will reach perfection—when you stand face-to-face with Jesus Christ.

This is described in 1 John 3:2–3:

> Dear friends, now we are children of God, and what
> we will be has not yet been made known. But we know
> that when he appears, we shall be like him, for we shall
> see him as he is. Everyone who has this hope in him
> purifies himself, just as he is pure. (NIV)

It will all come into focus on that final day when you
stand before Jesus Christ. It is then that you will be in that
perfect state you have been aiming for—but not until that
day.

God will complete this work He has begun in you.
There might be lapses. There might be times when you
stumble and fall. There might be times when you feel like
you are making no progress at all. But God will complete
His work.

That should bring joy to your heart. It means you don't
have to do it all. You just have to do the best that you can
and apply yourself to living this Christian life. God will
bring to completion the work He is doing in your life.

CHAPTER TWO

A Worthwhile Passion

What are you passionate about? What lights your fire? What makes you tick? Everyone is passionate about something. We all have someone or something that we live for, some passion or ideal that drives us on, giving our lives purpose.

What is your master passion? What gets your blood pumping? If you had to sum up what you actually live for in one or two phrases, what would you say?

Maybe you're waiting for something to happen. Maybe you're waiting for children to grow up and leave home … waiting to take that trip you've been dreaming about for so long … waiting to find a husband or wife … waiting for things to get better. Waiting for retirement … waiting for tomorrow.

The problem with this is that one day you will wake up and realize that you are quite a bit older. In fact, you will realize that you have more life behind you than you have in front of you. You will realize that because you have not focused on where you are going in life, there is a certain aimlessness about your existence, confirming the truth of the old adage that says if you aim at nothing, you are bound to hit it.

A Master Passion

The apostle Paul had a master passion in life. In Philippians 1, we discover what that was—what he lived for. It is what all believers should live for as well: "For to me, to live is Christ, and to die is gain" (v. 21). When you hear a statement like that, you might be thinking, *It is a nice sentiment to say, "To live is Christ," but I don't know how practical that is.*

Often when someone is perceived as a little too spiritually oriented for most tastes, he or she is criticized as being too heavenly minded to be any earthly good. But in most cases, I think you will find that those who have been the most heavenly minded actually have been the most earthly good. In fact, if you look at history, you will find that those who have done the most for this world have been the ones who have thought more of the next one.

Here in the United States, some of our great universities were founded by Bible-believing Christians with the intent of not only educating people, but also of teaching them about Jesus Christ. You might even be surprised to know that such institutions as Yale and Harvard have solid evangelical roots.

This is typical of the direction Christians wanting to make an impact on their culture have taken throughout history. They have started hospitals. They have established shelters. They have reached out to the downtrodden and the hurting in our world with the gospel of Christ, not only preaching to them, but also clothing them, feeding them, and taking care of them.

Even today, when a problem develops somewhere in the world such as a famine or natural disaster, it is Christians who are usually leading the way through relief efforts, trying to do something for people in need. I am not aware of any atheistic relief organizations.

So the truth is that if you are truly heavenly minded, then you will be of the greatest earthly good.

When Paul said, "To live is Christ," he was speaking of the fact that he had an interest in the things of this life. He looked forward to going to be with the Lord, but he recognized that he had a job to do: "But if I live on in the flesh, this will mean fruit from my labor; yet what I shall choose I cannot tell. For I am hard-pressed between the two … " (Phil. 1:22–23).

Authentic Christianity

Paul had a practical spirituality. While it's true that Paul loved Jesus and wanted to live for Him, it is also true that he was utterly human. Without question, he had a holy passion for the things of God. But he did not live in stained glass. He was a real person with the same struggles and passions that we have. We know from reading his life story in the Book of Acts that he had his conflicts. Even Paul got into disagreements with people.

We know that he would get upset at times. On one occasion when he was standing before the high priest on false charges, he said something to the high priest and was struck in the face. Furious, he told the high priest, "God will strike you, you whitewashed wall! For you sit to judge me according to the law, and do you command me to be struck contrary to the law?" (Acts 23:3). That doesn't sound like turning the other cheek to me—it sounds like something I might do.

Yet Paul didn't sit around with a death wish. I don't think anyone loved life more than Paul did. He was a practical man. When his life was threatened, he didn't walk out into the midst of the crowd and say, "Here I am! If you want to kill me, go ahead and do it!" We read in Acts 9 that in Damascus, the believers put him into a basket and lowered him over the city wall at night so he could escape the Jews who were plotting to kill him. Paul was practical. He wanted to live. But he had his priorities in order. His was a balanced spirituality.

The most godly men and women I have had the privilege of meeting over the years have always impressed me with a genuine spirituality. And I can assure you that the godliest people I know are real people. That is what I like about them. They love God. Their priorities are in order. Yet there is balance to their lives. Theirs is a practical faith, not a strange, unattainable kind of spirituality. It is this real faith that the Bible proclaims.

When Paul said, "To live is Christ, and to die is gain," he was not speaking of an elite spirituality that could be experienced only by him or by the first-century Christians. He was speaking of an experience, a lifestyle that should, quite literally, be the norm for every follower of Jesus Christ throughout history, from his day to ours.

I think we could safely assume that for many, if not most of the first-century believers, their motto for living was the same as Paul's: to live is Christ. There were no social advantages to being a Christian in those days. In fact, you could lose your very life as a result. Yet the way they impacted their culture is nothing short of breathtaking. The first-century Christians did not outargue the pagans; they outlived them.

However, it seems to me that the Christianity of the New Testament—first-century Christianity—indeed differs from the Christianity of today. I think that is because we as a contemporary church have strayed from God's original intent to a large degree.

It is worth noting that the Christians of the first century made no attempts to conquer paganism and dead Judaism by reacting blow-by-blow. Instead, the early believers outthought, outprayed, and outlived the unbelievers. Their weapons were positive, not negative. They did not conduct protests or organize boycotts. They did not put on campaigns in an attempt to unseat the Roman emperors. But they did pray, preach, and proclaim the message of Christ. And to a large degree, they won over a good portion of their culture. The first-century Christians, like Paul, could say, "To live is Christ." If we would say the same thing, we could impact our culture today in a much more effective way.

To Live Is …

We all live for something. We all can say, "To live is … " For some, to live is business. For others, to live is fun. You fill in the blank. But everyone lives for something.

Some would say, "To live is … to just live." In fact, their motto for life might be, "Live and let live." They just live to gratify their impulses. Paul describes people like this as having their appetites as their god (see Phil. 3:19). They just live for the moment. If they want to do something, they just do it. They don't contemplate the meaning of life, why they are here, or where they are going. They don't care about things like that. They don't want to get into any discussion about life and its meaning, because it makes them uncomfortable. They just want to keep the conversation light. They just live to live. This describes a lot of people today.

Then there are others who would say, "For me, to live is pleasure. I live for fun. I live for the weekend." They may live for a certain sport or hobby that isn't necessarily sinful. It could be a relatively innocent activity that has been raised from the level of something they do to something that controls them.

A lot of people are very passionate about sports. For them, to live is football. When it's football season, just try to pry them out of their recliner or grab their remote control. They are going to live, eat, and drink football. They are passionate about it.

For someone else, it might be golf. For another, it might be surfing or snowboarding. Whatever it may be, the common denominator is pleasure. When they do the thing they are passionate about, it gives them pleasure.

Then there are those who live for sinful pleasure. Maybe it is sexual immorality or some other thing they try to derive pleasure from. The Bible warns that if we do this, we will pay a price for it. Paul issued this warning: "But she who lives in pleasure is dead while she lives" (1 Timothy 5:6).

Another might say, "I don't live for pleasure; I live to acquire possessions." Their motto in life would be, "The one who dies with the most toys wins." The idea is to just get more and more stuff. King Solomon, a man of incredible wealth, shared his thoughts about this in the Book of Ecclesiastes. He said,

Whatever my eyes desired I did not keep from them. I did not withhold my heart from any pleasure, for my heart rejoiced in all my labor; and this was my reward from all my labor. Then I looked on all the works that my hands had done and on the labor in which I had

toiled; and indeed all was vanity and grasping for the wind. There was no profit under the sun.
(Eccl. 2:10–11 niv)

Someone else might say, "I am not into just living. I am not into the pursuit of pleasure or the acquiring of possessions. "For me," they would say, "to live is to acquire knowledge. To live is to get a good education and expand my mind." Certainly that is a more noble pursuit than the mere chasing after pleasures or possessions. It is good to pursue knowledge. It is great to get a fine education. But if in the process of doing that you leave out God, it will be an empty search, leading to a dead end.

Solomon had attained greatness. He gained more wisdom than all who were before him. But he said, "And I set my heart to know wisdom and to know madness and folly. I perceived that this also is grasping for the wind. For in much wisdom is much grief, and he who increases knowledge increases sorrow" (Eccl. 1:17–18). Solomon was commenting on the fact that if you pursue knowledge and leave out God, it is an empty search.

A Single Focus

Maybe you're thinking, *Well, Greg, none of this sounds like me. I don't live for possessions. I don't live for pleasure. I don't even live for knowledge, per se. I live for Christ.* I don't doubt your sincerity in that statement. You might be actively involved in your church. You might attend every week and even go to midweek studies. You might go to prayer meetings. You might be involved in sharing the gospel. But here is something to consider: it is possible to do those things and lose sight of your main objective. Maybe a more accurate statement would be, "To live is service," or "To live is going to church," or "To live is preaching the gospel."

Paul said, "To live is Christ." Preaching the gospel is obviously important. Serving the Lord is essential. But these things should be an outgrowth of living for Christ. Sometimes we get so involved with our schedules that we forget about Christ. We substitute work for worship and perspiration for inspiration.

You may be surprised to know that those who are in Christian service are in greater danger of falling into this trap than almost anyone else. We are like Martha who was "distracted with much serving" (Luke 10:40) and busy, busy, busy. We should be wise like her sister Mary, who recognized there was a time to sit at the feet of Jesus. We need to be able to truly say, "To live is Christ."

But what does that mean? For Paul, it meant that he was passionately committed to the Lord. He said, "But one thing I do: Forgetting what is behind and straining toward what is ahead, I press on toward the goal to win the prize for which God has called me heavenward in Christ Jesus" (Phil. 3:13–14 NIV). This was a man who knew where he was going. Formerly a leading Pharisee and a member of the elite Sanhedrin, Paul had his taste of pleasure and power and the empty pursuit of knowledge. Looking back on all that, he said,

> But whatever was to my profit I now consider loss for the sake of Christ. What is more, I consider everything a loss compared to the surpassing greatness of knowing Christ Jesus my Lord, for whose sake I have lost all things. I consider them rubbish, that I may gain Christ. (Phil. 3:7–8 NIV)

Paul essentially was saying, "I have accomplished a lot. All of that power, all of that prestige, all of that education I once valued so highly means nothing to me now, because it actually was keeping me from Christ. It is refuse. It is rubbish. All that matters to me is Jesus."

Paul never lost sight of the encounter he had with the Lord on the Damascus Road. The great apostle Paul once was the wicked Saul of Tarsus. As a member of the Sanhedrin, he presided over the death of Stephen, the courageous young man who laid down his life for the gospel. Saul hunted down and arrested Christians wherever he found them, believing that he was doing the work of God in the process. So imagine his surprise when on the Damascus Road, he met none other than the risen Christ. You might say that Paul spent the rest of his life discovering who Jesus was and what He wanted him to do. This was a man who could honestly say, "To live is Christ."

The Reality of Mortality

Only the man or woman who can say, "To live is Christ," can also say, as Paul said, "To die is gain." Death is a subject many people are uncomfortable with. They don't like to deal with it. They like to pretend it will never happen, but indeed it will.

When Meryl Streep celebrated her 50th birthday, she commented, "All I want is more time. That's what I want, and nobody can give me that as a present, all wrapped up with a ribbon."[2]

On her deathbed, Elizabeth I, Queen of England, said, "All my possessions for a moment of time." But that royal request was not granted, because even queens die.

No one can give us more time, and we don't know when our lives will end. Medical science attempts to add years to our lives, but only Jesus Christ can add life to our years and give us a life that is worth living. Only Jesus Christ can give us the guaranteed hope that when we die, we will immediately go into His presence.

Paul recognized that being with Christ was a certainty. It was a part of life—not the conclusion of it. It was the beginning—not an ending. It was life on a far greater and better level. It was a promotion. A coronation. A reward. He said, "If I am to go on living in the body, this will mean fruitful labor for me. Yet what shall I choose? I do not know! I am torn between the two: I desire to depart and be with Christ, which is better by far" (Phil. 1:22–23 NIV). In the original language, the word Paul used for "depart" is an interesting one. It could be translated, "to break camp" or "to strike the tent."

I am not a major fan of camping. I like it for a few hours. But I enjoy the comforts of home even more. I like clean clothes and that thing called the shower. Some people just love camping, however. They want to get out there in nature, lie in the dirt, build the fire, and kill the food. I like to break camp. That is good news to me, because it means I am out of there.

Paul was saying, "I am ready to break camp. I am ready to pull up the stakes for this old tent." Writing to the church at Corinth on the subject of death, Paul said, "For we know that if our earthly house, this tent, is destroyed, we have a building from God, a house not made with hands, eternal in the heavens" (2 Corinthians 5:1). I find it interesting that the Bible compares our bodies to a tent. It's a good illustration, because tents are a temporary residence, not a permanent home. Tents get old, wear out, and wrinkle just like our bodies do.

The Hope of Heaven

Another meaning behind this word "depart" is the idea of untying a boat from its moorings and setting sail.

Whether or not you are happy about setting sail really depends on where you are going. Imagine that you have a friend named John who is going on a trip. He will be boarding a freighter to outer Siberia in the middle of winter. You go down to the dock and wave goodbye to John, who is bundled up in all his clothes. You are thinking to yourself, *Poor John. I feel so sorry for him. It will be tough there in outer Siberia.*

But let's say that instead of a freighter, John was going on a boat, and it was a cruise ship to Tahiti. As you stand on the dock waving goodbye to John, you are thinking, *Poor me. I am still here, but John is going to Tahiti.*

That is the picture Paul was painting when he said, "I desire to depart and be with Christ, which is better by far." Paul was saying, "I am setting sail. I am going to a better place." But it is a place much better than Tahiti. Paul was going to heaven to be with Christ. Paul wasn't necessarily in a rush to get there. But he knew it was a better place to be.

It is like the little boy who was listening to his pastor preaching about going to heaven. The pastor asked the congregation, "How many of you would like to go to heaven tonight?" Everyone's hand shot up except the little boy's. So the pastor asked the question again: "How many of you would like to go to heaven tonight?" Again, every hand went up but one. So the pastor stopped, looked at the little boy, and said, "Son, don't you want to go to heaven?"

"Yes … someday," the boy answered. "But I thought you were getting up a load right now!"

Paul wanted to go to heaven, but he didn't have a death wish. He simply recognized that when the time came for him to depart, heaven would be far better than his life on Earth. Here's why:

1. Heaven is better, because we are moving from a tent to a mansion. This is the very picture Scripture paints for us. Instead of living in our corruptible, aging bodies, we will be given new bodies: incorruptible, perfect, and without any sinful inclinations or depraved natures. Paul said, "For the perishable must clothe itself with the imperishable, and the mortal with immortality. When the perishable has been clothed with the imperishable, and the mortal with immortality, then the saying that is written will come true: 'Death has been swallowed up in victory' " (1 Corinthians 15:53–54 NIV).

2. Heaven is better, because there will be no suffering or death. Revelation 21:3–4 tells us, " 'Now the dwelling of God is with men, and he will live with them. They will be his people, and God himself will be with them and be their God. He will wipe every tear from their eyes. There will be no more death or mourning or crying or pain, for the old order of things has passed away' " (NIV).

3. Heaven is better, because it will be immediate. Notice Paul said, "I desire to depart and be with Christ," not "I desire to depart and go into a holding area," or "I desire to depart and go to purgatory," or "I desire to depart and go into a soul sleep." Paul said none of those things, because he knew that the moment he took his last breath on Earth, he would take his first breath in heaven.

He would go immediately into the presence of God. In 2 Corinthians 5:8, he pointed out that to be absent from the body is to be present with the Lord.

4. Heaven is better, because in heaven all of our questions will be answered. We are told in 1 Corinthians 13:12, "Now we see things imperfectly as in a cloudy mirror, but then we will see everything with perfect clarity. All that I know now is partial and incomplete, but then I will know everything completely, just as God now knows me completely" (NLT).

5. Heaven is better, because we will be with Christ. This is all that really mattered to Paul. He wanted to be with

We substitute work for worship and perspiration for inspiration.

the Lord. It is great that we will have new bodies. It is wonderful that our questions will be answered. It is comforting to know there will be no more pain or suffering or sorrow. But what really matters is that we will be with Jesus.

The great evangelist D. L. Moody said, "It is not the jeweled walls and the pearly gates that are going to make heaven attractive. It is being with God." Being with Jesus—that is the hope of every Christian.

What do you live for? If you say, "To live is money," then for you to die is to leave it all behind. If you say, "To live is fame," then for you to die is to be forgotten. If you say, "To live is power," then for you to die is to lose it all. But if you can say, "To live is Christ," then you will be able to say that to die is gain. This is not bizarre spirituality, but down-to-earth, practical, lifechanging, New Testament Christianity. That is what God wants for us.

I find it interesting how people can get fired up over their favorite sports team, faithfully watching every game, wearing the team's colors, and even painting their faces—and we think nothing of it, other than assuming they really must love their team. But when it comes to Christianity, if someone reads the Bible on a regular basis, attends church faithfully, or even lifts his or her hands in a worship service, such a person is considered a fanatic.

So maybe we need a little more fanaticism—not crazy, out-of-control zeal, but a passionate desire for the Lord Jesus Christ in which we have as much—or better yet, more—passion for Him as we have for these other things in life.

Do you have that for Him right now? It's easy to just mouth the words: "To live is Christ." But is it true? Is it a passion for the Lord that keeps you going? Or is it something else?

Other pursuits are not necessarily bad. But if they are more important to you than Jesus, then they can be bad. They can even become idols in your life.

As Christians, we need to always remember that the main thing is to keep the main thing the main thing. The main thing is Jesus. And we all should be able to say, "To live is Christ."

CHAPTER THREE

The Upside-Down Principle

Everyone wants to be happy. But are we? A 2005 poll conducted by the Pew Research Center revealed that just one-third, or 34 percent, of adults in the U.S. said they were "very happy." Another 50 percent acknowledged they were "pretty happy," while 15 percent stated they were "not too happy." And one percent of those polled didn't know whether they were happy or not.[3]

While we want to be happy and fulfilled, the fact of the matter is that the true and lasting happiness we are searching for in life will not come from some formula that our culture offers us.

The problem with happiness is that it is entirely contingent on good things happening. When things are going well, we are happy. When things are not going well, we are not happy.

Isn't it amazing how you can go from one emotion to another so quickly? Maybe you're happy because you're doing well in your job, even making a little extra money. But all of the sudden you lose the job. Or all of the sudden an unexpected bill comes in. Then you are not happy. Or maybe you're happy and feeling well. But then you get sick. Suddenly you are unhappy.

Conventional wisdom says that if you want to be happy, then you need to look out for number one. You need to get out there and do whatever it takes to succeed, whatever it takes to fulfill your own desires and needs. It doesn't matter whom you step on. It doesn't matter who gets hurt in the process. You have to think about yourself. At least, that is what the world tells us.

The question is, does this formula work? No, it does not. Because all of us, having tried this formula to some degree, know that it is a complete failure. We know that this kind of happiness ebbs and flows with circumstances and doesn't last.

God's Formula

God offers us something better than this brand of happiness. But His formula runs in a contradictory manner to what the world tells us. The Bible speaks of something called joy that can be experienced by the Christian, the person who has put his or her faith in Jesus Christ. This is one of the primary themes of the Book of Philippians. Again and again, it speaks of joy. In fact, the theme of joy is repeated nineteen times in this relatively short book. Throughout its four chapters, Paul mentions joy, rejoicing, and gladness. Philippians is a book about joyful living. And it is in Philippians that we find God's formula for a meaningful and full life:

> Therefore if there is any consolation in Christ, if any comfort of love, if any fellowship of the Spirit, if any affection and mercy, fulfill my joy by being like-minded, having the same love, being of one accord, of one mind. Let nothing be done through selfish ambition or conceit, but in lowliness of mind let each esteem others

better than himself. Let each of you look out not only for his own interests, but also for the interests of others. (Phil. 2:1–4)

Does this not go against the conventional wisdom of how to succeed and be happy in life? Everyone says, "Look out for yourself. Think of yourself." But the Bible says, "Don't look out for yourself. Don't look out for your own interests, but the interests of others."

The Myth of Self-Love

With all the emphasis in our culture today on the importance of self-love, self-worth, self-image, and self-esteem, how different the Bible is. What really bothers me is that we even hear these ideas being propagated from the pulpits of our churches at times. Ministers will get up and say, "You need more self-love. You need a greater sense of self-esteem. You need a better self-image." But the Bible does not teach that.

The Bible teaches that we already love ourselves. We already look out for number one. That comes with human nature; it isn't something we need to learn how to do.

Some have taught that because the Bible says, " 'You shall love your neighbor as yourself' " (Matt. 19:19; 22:39; Mark 12:31), then you need to love yourself. Before you can love your neighbor, they say, you must first learn to love yourself.

But Jesus is not saying you need to learn to love yourself so you can love your neighbor. He is simply saying that you already love yourself—that is obvious, a no-brainer. Therefore, love your neighbor as much as you love yourself.

We don't need to learn how to love self; we need to learn how to deny self. That is what the Bible teaches. Jesus said, "If anyone desires to come after Me, let him deny himself, and take up his cross, and follow Me" (Matt. 16:24). Here is the twist: "For whoever desires to save his life will lose it, but whoever loses his life for My sake will find it" (Matt.16:24).

This is upside down from what our culture says, which is, "Look for self-fulfillment and you will find it." But the Bible says that if you look for that, you will never find it. Try the acronym JOY:

J – Jesus
O – Others
Y – Yourself

Put God first, others second, and yourself third, and you will find joy. It is the upside-down life.

However, we tend to follow the acronym YOJ. We put self first, others second, and then maybe fit God in there somewhere. It is the me-first mentality so prevalent in our culture.

Him First

The Bible gives an account of one man who, when Jesus said, "Follow Me," responded, "Lord, let me first go and bury my father" (Luke 9:59). His words exposed his problem: "Lord, … me first." That doesn't work. He had it all mixed up. If He is Lord, then it is Him first.

The Bible teaches that we are to put God and others first. No one has modeled this more perfectly for us than Jesus Christ. If ever there was someone who walked this earth who deserved to be waited on hand and foot, it was Jesus. If ever there was someone who could justly demand

His own rights, it was Jesus. Yet He modeled incredible humility and gave us an example to follow. Philippians 2:5–7 tells us,

> Let this mind be in you which was also in Christ Jesus, who, being in the form of God, did not consider it robbery to be equal with God, but made Himself of no reputation, taking the form of a bondservant, and coming in the likeness of men.

Notice verse 5: "Let this mind be in you which was also in Christ Jesus … " Here is the pattern we are to follow, the example of Jesus Christ himself: we need to have the mind of Christ.

The Servant-Leader

John 13 provides us with a wonderful illustration of what the mind of Christ is. As all the disciples were gathered together for a meal, Jesus did something quite unexpected: He took off His outer garment, got down on His hands and knees, took a basin of water and a towel, and began to wash the feet of each and every disciple.

Peter was so amazed at this that he basically said, "Lord, You can't wash my feet! This is crazy!"

But Jesus told him, "If I do not wash you, you have no part with Me" (John 13:8). At that point Peter wanted a bath. Here was Jesus himself, God Almighty, the Creator of the Universe, on His hands and knees washing the feet of His disciples. But He didn't just wash Peter's feet or John's feet or James' feet. He washed the feet of Judas, the one who would betray him. I would not have washed Judas' feet. But I would have seriously considered drowning him in the pan. Yet Jesus did no such thing.

Paul was not speaking of imitation, but impartation.

Instead, He set an example of servanthood for all of us to see.

If you want to live a joyful life, if you want to live a fulfilled life, then you need to follow the example of Jesus. And in addition to His example, God has given us a pattern for joy in Philippians. In chapter 1, Paul said, "To live is Christ and to die is gain." This means we put Jesus first.

Then in chapter 2, he tells us to put others' needs above our own: "Let nothing be done through selfish ambition or conceit, but in lowliness of mind let each esteem others better than himself. Let each of you look out not only for his own interests, but also for the interests of others" (vv. 3–4). This means we put others second. Then we put ourselves third.

An Unexpected Outcome

The great joy that comes from having the mind of Christ, which is loving the unlovable and giving out what God has given to us, is finding the overflowing joy that results.

"Remember the words of the Lord Jesus," Acts 20:35 reminds us, "that He said, 'It is more blessed to give than to receive.' " Children don't get that. They think it is more blessed to get than to give. One of the first words they learn is "mine." Just watch two kids when one picks up a toy that the other wants. That orientation toward self has been there from birth. That is why we have to teach our children to share. Then, as the years pass and they reach adulthood, they start realizing it is a joy to give.

I love to give presents, and I love to give them more than get them. My problem is that when I have a gift to give, I can't wait. When I start Christmas shopping for my wife and children, I want to give them their gifts as soon as I buy them. I don't like to wait. I like to give the gifts because it brings me pleasure. It is more blessed to give than to receive.

We could apply that principle to life in general. Instead of worrying about some trivial issue, what about reaching out to someone who is in desperate need? Getting your eyes off yourself and thinking about someone else could change your life. When you are doing something for another person, you forget about yourself in the process. All of the sudden you discover that as you are helping, blessing, and reaching out to others, you are happy. Where did it come from? I can tell you that it didn't come from the pursuit of your own pleasure. It came from forgetting about yourself and putting the needs of others above your own. That is what Paul meant when he said, "Let this mind be in you which was also in Christ Jesus" (Phil. 2:5).

Not Imitation, but Impartation

Paul was not speaking of imitation, but impartation. In other words, you can say, "I will let this mind be in me which was also in Christ. I will be like Christ as much as I possibly can. I will try to follow His moral example." But let's not forget that Philippians was written to believers, to Christians. These are not words for all humanity to live by; these are words written to followers of Jesus Christ.

The only way that I can be like Jesus is by His giving me a new nature. In other words, when He comes and forgives me of my sin and lives inside me, I have new desires as a result. That is impartation.

I cannot do this stuff on my own, which is imitation. I can't love unlovable people on my own. I can love people that I like, but I can't love people that I don't like. That is something I need God's help with. I cannot reach out to someone and not think about myself. I need God's help to do that.

Maybe you have tried to be a religious person. You've thought, *If only I could be moral and live by these standards and follow the example of Jesus.* ... But unless you are a Christian, you won't be able to do that. You need God's help. You need to come to Him and say, "I have tried on my own. I need Your help. I need Your forgiveness."

The Case for Humility

The simple fact is that sooner or later, everyone will bow the knee to Jesus Christ. You might be thinking, *You Christians might, but not me.* I have news for you, friend. You will bow too. Everyone will. This is what the Bible teaches:

> Therefore God also has highly exalted Him and given Him the name which is above every name, that at the name of Jesus every knee should bow, of those in heaven, and of those on earth, and of those under the earth, and that every tongue should confess that Jesus Christ is Lord, to the glory of God the Father. (Phil. 2:9–11)

You can either bow and confess your sins and be forgiven now, or you will bow later and acknowledge what is obvious. But then it will be too late. Now is by choice. Later will be by command.

Today you have a choice in the matter. You can choose to bow to Jesus. Or, you can say, "I am not going to bow. I am going to do what I want to do." Then you will bow later, because when you stand before God Almighty on that final day, you will bow. But here is the problem: It will be too late then. It will be an acknowledgement in that final day, but not something you did willfully on this side of heaven. That is why you need to do it now.

Would you like to meet the living Jesus, the one who humbled himself and died on the cross for your sins? If so, then you need to humble yourself and admit your need for Him. The Bible says, "So humble yourselves under the mighty power of God, and at the right time he will lift you up in honor. Give all your worries and cares to God, for he cares about you" (1 Peter 5:6–7 NLT).

Maybe you have been thinking about becoming a Christian and have been looking into the whole "Christianity thing." "I am slowly in the process of converting," you might say.

But that is not the way it works. Either you are converted or you are not. Either you are a believer or you are not. Either you have said yes to Jesus, or you have said no. Until you have said yes, you are saying no by default. Is that where you want to be?

It isn't enough to admire Jesus or to think well of Jesus. He said He was God. He said He was the only way to the Father, the only way for you to be forgiven, and the only way to heaven. Either you will accept that or you won't.

It is time to get serious and follow Jesus. When you do, you will discover that the upside-down life is truly worth living.

CHAPTER 4

An Example Worth Following

The example of servanthood and humility Jesus set for us during His earthly life is nothing short of amazing. But equally amazing is the fact that God became a man. Though I've heard it said many times and have studied it quite extensively, the thought that Jesus became a man and walked among us remains truly mind-boggling to me.

I can read about a God in heaven who loves me. I can read about a flawless, perfect, and holy God, and that moves me. But it can be hard to relate to a God like that.

It is like the little boy who was frightened one stormy night. As the lightning cracked outside, he called out from his room to his father and said, "Daddy, I am scared!"

"Son, don't worry," the father said from the other room. "God loves you, and He will take care of you."

The little boy answered, "I know God loves me, but right now I want someone who has skin on!"

God with Skin On

Jesus was God with skin on. He walked among us as a man. But during this earthly ministry of Jesus, many of the people were perplexed about who He really was. The Pharisees were asked, "What do you think about the Christ? Whose Son is He?" (Matt. 22:41). To some degree, even His disciples were perplexed. I don't think they fully grasped His mission and who He was until His death and resurrection. When Jesus was walking the earth, some thought He was Jeremiah the prophet. Others thought He was Elijah. King Herod actually thought that He was John the Baptist back from the dead. To this very day, people are still confused about who He was.

Ironically, there has never been a time when more people profess faith in Him, yet at the same time do not know who He really was. The problem is that people will say they believe in Jesus. They will say they are Christians and that they love God. But in no way do their lives follow the pattern of what a Christian should be living for. Maybe they don't believe in the same Jesus I believe in. Maybe they don't even understand who Jesus was.

> **Jesus did not say, "Admire Me" or "Think well of Me." He said, "Follow Me."**

Pontius Pilate, who tried Jesus, said, "I find no fault in this man" (Luke 23:4). He was faced with a question that everyone is ultimately faced with, which is, "What then shall I do with Jesus who is called Christ?" (Matt. 27:22).

Napoleon Bonaparte said of Him, "I know men and I tell you, Jesus Christ is no mere man." French historian Ernest Renan said, "All history is incomprehensible without Christ." H. G. Wells said, "Christ is the most unique person of history. No man can write a history of the human race without giving first and foremost place to the penniless teacher of Nazareth."[4] John Stuart Mill described Jesus "in the very first rank of the men of sublime genius of whom our species can boast."[5] And British social reformer Robert Owen called Him "the irreproachable." [6]

Yet all of these titles and descriptions fall short of identifying the real Jesus. He was more than just a model of religion or the most unique person in history. He was the man who was God. He was the Messiah of Israel. He was the Savior of the world. He is the only man who ever was God—not a man who became God, which is impossible, but He was God who became a man. And it is an event never to be repeated again. So we each must make a decision concerning Him. As C. S. Lewis so wisely observed, "You must make your choice. Either this man was, and is, the Son of God: or else a madman or something worse...."[7]

Jesus did not say, "Admire Me" or "Think well of Me." He said, "Follow Me." But there are many who say things like, "That Jesus, He was a wonderful prophet. He was a great, godly man." No, He was more than that. He made radical claims. Jesus claimed to be God in human form. What's more, He claimed to be the only way to have a relationship with God the Father. The question is whether you believe that or reject that. There are no other options.

Jesus never became God, nor did He ever cease to be God. His deity, which means His divine Lordship, the fact that He was God, was pre-human, pre-earthly, and pre-Mary. He was God before He was born in a stable in Bethlehem. And He remained God after He became a man and walked this earth. So if you're wondering whether Jesus laid aside His deity at the point of the Incarnation, when he came to this earth and was born of the Virgin Mary, the answer is no. He also remained God when He was resurrected and ascended into heaven. Never for a moment did Jesus cease being God Almighty. It is hard for us to understand, but it is simply true.

Philippians 2 tells us that Jesus, "being in the form of God, did not consider it robbery to be equal with God, but made Himself of no reputation, taking the form of a bondservant, and coming in the likeness of men. And being found in appearance as a man, He humbled Himself and became obedient to the point of death, even the death of the cross (vv. 6–8).

Charles Wesley put it well in his Christmas carol, "Hark the Herald Angels Sing," when he wrote, "Veiled in flesh the Godhead see, hail the incarnate Deity! Pleased as man with men to dwell, Jesus, our Emmanuel." *Veiled in flesh the Godhead see. …* Jesus never voided His deity, but He did veil it. We are given a glimpse of this in the story of His transfiguration, when Jesus took Peter, James, and John up a mountain. They fell asleep, as they often did at very critical times. And when they awoke, there was Jesus, with Moses and Elijah standing on each side of Him. The Bible says His garments shined like the sun. Now it was not a miracle that Jesus shined like the sun that day during His transfiguration. The real miracle was that He didn't shine like that all the time. There for a moment, He let Peter, James, and John see who He really was. He was indeed God, but He veiled His glory.

Jesus never voided His deity; He veiled it. As C. H. Spurgeon said, He was "infinite, and an infant. Eternal, and yet born of a woman. Almighty, and yet hanging on a woman's breast. Supporting a universe, and yet needing to be carried in a mother's arms. King of angels, and yet the reputed son of Joseph. Heir of all things, and yet the carpenter's despised son."

It can all be adequately summed up in 2 Corinthians 8:9: "For you know the grace of our Lord Jesus Christ, that though he was rich, yet for your sakes he became poor, so that you through his poverty might become rich" (NIV). Jesus went from the throne of heaven to a feeding trough. He went from the presence of angels into a cold, dark cave filled with animals. He who was larger than the universe became an embryo. He who sustains the world with a word chose to be dependent upon the nourishment of a young girl. God became a fetus. The Almighty appeared on Earth as a helpless human baby, unable to do anything but lie and stare and wiggle and make noises, needing to be fed, changed, and taught to walk like any other child. The more you think about it, the more staggering it gets that God became a man—and that God became a baby.

The Question of the Virgin Birth

By the way, belief in the Virgin Birth is not optional; it is essential to being a Christian. Why is it so important? Consider this: It is the way God decided to come to this earth. He could have chosen other ways, but this is the way He chose.

It would no doubt have been possible for Jesus to come to this earth as a complete, yet sinless, human being without a human bearing Him. In other words, He could have just appeared: "I'm here—God in human form." He wouldn't have had to go through the entire process of being born in Bethlehem and being raised in the home of Mary and Joseph. He could have appeared as a full-grown man and said, "Here I am. I have arrived." If He had done it that way, He would be sinless, but He would seem unapproachable. He wouldn't seem human. It would be difficult for us to believe He was a human being like us.

On the other hand, He could have been born to two human parents, and God could have supernaturally intervened and caused Him to be without sin. But then there would have been the nagging doubt that maybe He is not divine after all.

God chose the right way. No other way would have accomplished His goal. His was the logical way. And when you really stop and think about it, it makes complete sense.

While it's true that a virgin birth is impossible—in human terms—Jesus himself said, "The things which are impossible with men are possible with God" (Luke 18:27). Of course the Virgin Birth was a miracle. It was an out-of-the-ordinary occurrence carried out by the hand of God.

If you believe that God can do what He says and that He has miracle-working power, then you can believe in the Virgin Birth. You can also believe in the resurrection of Christ as well as the miracles brought forth by Jesus.

On the other hand, if you don't believe in the Virgin Birth, then it means that you don't believe what God says. It also means that you don't believe He can do miracles. Jesus said, "If you do not believe that I am He, you will die in your sins" (John 8:24). Any Scripture-believing Jew of Jesus' day would have understood the significance of that statement. They would have remembered the conversation between God and Moses at the burning bush. Moses said, "If I go to the people of Israel and tell them, 'The God of your ancestors has sent me to you,' they will ask me, 'What is his name?' Then what should I tell them?" (Ex. 3:13 NLT).

God answered, "I Am Who I Am. Say this to the people of Israel: I Am has sent me to you" (v. 14 NLT).

So when Jesus said, "If you do not believe that I am, ..." He was equating himself with God. Essentially He was saying that unless we believe He is equal with God, we will die in our sins. So you see, belief in the Virgin Birth is necessary for being a true believer.

The Deity of Jesus

Some would assert that Jesus never really claimed to be God. But as a matter of fact, He did. For one, we have the statement I just mentioned from John 8:34: "If you do not believe that I am He, you will die in your sins." This was a clear statement of equality with the Father.

Also on many occasions He accepted worship, something that was reserved for God alone. In fact, when Jesus was tempted by the devil in the wilderness, He quoted Scripture, saying, " 'You shall worship the Lord your God, and Him only you shall serve' " (Matt. 4:10). Jesus was underscoring the fact that worship is to be given to God alone. Yet Jesus accepted worship on many occasions. If He wasn't God, then He would have stopped people in their tracks when they began to worship Him.

When an angel revealed truths to the apostle John that he would later record in the Book of Revelation, John was so overwhelmed that he fell down to worship the angel. But the angel said, "See that you do not do that! I am your fellow servant, and of your brethren who have the testimony of Jesus. Worship God!" (Rev. 19:10).

Yet Jesus accepted worship. After His resurrection, when He appeared before Thomas in the Upper Room, Thomas exclaimed, "My Lord and my God!" (John 20:28) and worshiped Him. If Jesus was not God, then He would have stopped Thomas and reminded him that it was blasphemy. But Jesus accepted the worship of Thomas because He was indeed God.

We also read Gospel accounts of Jesus' forgiving sins, and only God can forgive sins. Matthew, Mark, and Luke record the story of the paralyzed man who was lowered through the ceiling of a house where Jesus was speaking. When Jesus saw the commitment of the man and his friends who went to so much effort, He looked at him (no doubt with a smile on His face) and said, "Son, be of good cheer; your sins are forgiven you" (Matt. 9:1). That really sent the Pharisees into an uproar. They said, "Who is this who speaks blasphemies? Who can forgive sins but God alone?" (Luke 5:21).

Jesus could have said, "That is true. Never mind. Skip that." But instead of doing that, Jesus said,

> "Which is easier, to say to the paralytic, 'Your sins are forgiven you,' or to say, 'Arise, take up your bed and walk'? But that you may know that the Son of Man has power on earth to forgive sins"—He said to the paralytic, "I say to you, arise, take up your bed, and go to your house." (Mark 2:9–11)

When the Pharisees asked, "Who can forgive sins but God alone?" Jesus basically said, "OK, I'm going to forgive his sins. I'm going to heal him, too, because I am God."

Throughout the Gospels we read how the Pharisees plotted against Jesus, seeking to kill Him, because He said God was His Father. He was, therefore, continually making himself equal with God. Without a doubt, Jesus claimed to be God.

Don't let anyone tell you that Jesus never claimed to be God. This, by the way, is one of the earmarks of a cult. When someone comes knocking at your door, ready to awaken you to some new spiritual truth, ask him or her who Jesus was. Was He the Son of God and God the

Son, the only true God? Is Jesus the only way to God the Father? If a person does not believe in the deity of Christ, then he or she adheres to a cultic belief. To be a true Christian, it is essential to believe that Jesus claimed to be God and indeed was God.

The Humanity of Jesus

Jesus was God. However, He accepted the limitations of humanity. We see this throughout the Gospels. We know that Jesus was tired. On one occasion, as He came to the city of Samaria, we are told that He was weary (see John 4:6). He had been walking all day, probably under Israel's scorching sun. Now, if I were God, I probably would not have done that. I would have said to the disciples, "You guys go on up to Samaria. I will see you there." Then I would have just appeared there. Why tire yourself out when you could just airlift yourself around? Jesus was God, after all. But He voluntarily went through the process of being tired and exhausted.

We know also that Jesus experienced physical hunger. During His temptation in the wilderness after fasting for forty days, the Bible says He was hungry (see Matt. 4:2).

In the Garden of Gethsemane, He said to Peter, James, and John, "My soul is exceedingly sorrowful, even to death. Stay here and watch with Me" (Matt. 26:38). Luke's Gospel adds this detail: "And being in agony, He prayed more earnestly. Then His sweat became like great drops of blood falling down to the ground" (Luke 26:43). Jesus was essentially saying to them, "Would you just be with Me right now?" It sounds as though He was experiencing loneliness. And I have no doubt that He experienced loneliness when He hung the cross, the sin of the world poured upon Him, and said, "My God, My God, why have You forsaken Me?" (Matt. 27:46; Mark 15:34). Momentarily, He was indeed forsaken by God.

We know that He experienced physical weakness, because when He was on the way to Calvary, bearing His cross, He fell beneath its weight. Having already had His back shredded open by the Roman cat-o'-nine-tails, He had lost a lot of blood. Under the weight of that tremendous beam, He collapsed to the ground.

We know that He experienced physical thirst. As He hung on the cross, the very God who created water, the very God who could speak to a rock and have water come gushing out, said, "I thirst!" (John 19:28).

Jesus knew what it was like to be weary. He knew what it was like to be hungry and thirsty. He knew what it was like to be lonely. He experienced all of those things. Hebrews 4:15 says that He "understands our weaknesses, for he faced all of the same testings we do, yet he did not sin" (NLT).

So the next time you are tired, hungry, thirsty, weary, or lonely, know that you have a God who knows what it is like to stand in your shoes. He is the only one who can accurately say, "I feel your pain." He was the God-Man. He walked this earth in a human body. He died like a man in the sense that His body ceased to function just like our bodies will when we die.

But Jesus also had a human mind. We don't really know whether he had the full knowledge of God while He was that little baby in the manger at Bethlehem. Just imagine if He had turned to Mary and said, "I am God in human form. By the way, Mary, Earth is round. Some people will say it is flat, but I am telling you it is round.

I made it myself." But He didn't do that. He squealed and giggled and made noises like any other baby would.

We don't know when this knowledge came to Him, but Luke 2:40 tells us, "And the Child grew and became strong in spirit, filled with wisdom; and the grace of God was upon Him." On one occasion, Joseph and Mary "found Him in the temple, sitting in the midst of the teachers, both listening to them and asking them questions" (v. 46).

Luke 2:52 says that "Jesus increased in wisdom and stature, and in favor with God and men." This would appear that Jesus went through a learning process like anyone else would. Yet at the same time, He did not have the limitations that sin brings into one's life. But it would seem, although we can't know for sure, that Jesus, though God, still experienced the limitations that accompanied physical and mental growth.

But just because Jesus possessed divine attributes such as omniscience and omnipotence does not mean that He could not have had a relatively normal human development. Could He not have possessed those qualities and yet chose not to use them? I think that's where the answer is: Yes, He possessed them, but He chose not to use them. There was never a moment in which He suddenly became God, when deity was transferred upon Him. That was always a part of His life.

The One Who Feels Our Pain

So not only did Jesus experience the physical limitations of a human body, but we also know that He experienced very real human emotion. In the familiar story of the resurrection of Lazarus from the dead, we see Him experiencing a broad range of human emotions. Jesus often spent time in Bethany with Lazarus, Mary, and Martha. But when word came that His friend Lazarus was sick, He intentionally delayed His arrival. By the time He arrived in Bethany, Lazarus was dead—so dead, in fact, that he had been in the tomb for four days. Martha wasted no time in getting to the point: "Lord, if You had been here, my brother would not have died" (John 11:21). Not much later, Mary arrived and repeated the same thing. Both were saying, for all practical purposes, "Lord, You let us down. You failed us."

No doubt this was a great disappointment to Jesus. He would have hoped they had more faith in Him, having spent so much time with Him—especially Mary, who sat at His feet and drank in His every word.

The Bible tells us that "when Jesus saw her weeping, and the Jews who came with her weeping, He groaned in the spirit and was troubled" (v. 33). And then we come to the shortest verse in the Bible: "Jesus wept" (v. 35). Tears fell down His cheeks.

And after His triumphal entry into Jerusalem, when the crowds were whipped into a frenzy, Jesus wept again. While everyone was thrilled and rejoicing, Jesus was sad and burdened as He knew, because He was all-knowing, that it wouldn't be long until the very people who were crying out, "Hosanna to the Son of David!" would be shouting, "Crucify Him, crucify Him!" His unexpected show of emotion must have shattered the stereotype of an angry, disinterested God. Here was Jesus, weeping for the people.

His earthly ministry was almost over at that point. Time was short. Yet by and large, He was rejected. Though He healed the sick, raised the dead, fed the hungry, and forgave sins, He remained mostly alone and rejected. As Isaiah 53:3 says, "He is despised and rejected by men, a Man of sorrows and acquainted with grief."

Attitude Adjustment Required

Jesus, who emptied Himself of the privileges of deity and walked among us as a man, set the example for us in how we should live. The Bible tells us, "Let this mind be in you which was also in Christ Jesus ..." (Phil. 2:5). Another way to translate this verse is, "Have this same attitude." That is not some mystical, unreachable goal; it is profoundly practical and applicable. It is simply saying that if you want to have the same mind as Jesus did, then you should seek the will of God above everything else. The same passage tells us, "Let nothing be done through selfish ambition or conceit, but in lowliness of mind let each esteem others better than himself. Let each of you look out not only for his own interests, but also for the interests of others" (vv. 3–4). In context, we see these statements building and then culminating in Jesus as an example of one who humbled himself. As His followers, we are to humble ourselves as well.

Refusing to follow Jesus' example of humility can lead to a devastating outcome. Remember, Satan, or Lucifer, was once a high-ranking angel in the presence of God. Yet he wasn't satisfied to worship God. He wanted to be worshiped as God. He wanted the top job. He wanted to be on the throne. He said, "I will ascend above the heights of the clouds, I will be like the Most High" (Isa. 14:14). While Lucifer said, "I will," Jesus said, "Thy will," as in "Thy will be done" (see Matt. 6:10). Lucifer was not satisfied to be a creation; he wanted to be the Creator. Yet Jesus, who was the Creator, willingly became a man.

There are so many today who want their own will, not God's. They want God to fit into their plans, saying, "Here is what I am going to do with my life. Here is what I am planning for my future ... for my career ... for my choice of a partner in life. ... Here is what I have decided. ... Lord, just bless it." But it doesn't work that way.

If you want to live life to its fullest, then live it God's way. Jesus said, "If you cling to your life, you will lose it; but if you give up your life for me, you will find it" (Matt. 10:39 NLT).

If you want to find yourself, then lose yourself. If you want to find your reason for being here, then submit your will to God, and you will discover that His plan for you is better than your plan for yourself.

If you don't believe this, then go out and make a mess of it, and after you have thrown away fifteen or twenty years, you will realize the error of your ways. Or worse yet, your heart will become so irreparably hardened that you will never turn back. But sooner or later, you will see that God's way was the right way.

You can either take God's word for it, or you can go out on your own and try to prove that He is wrong. It is a better lesson to learn that what God says is for our own good. These standards, these rules that He has given us in Scripture, are there for our protection. They are there to bless us and enrich us.

Some might say, "Well, I don't really do humility." But as one theologian put it, "The world's a better place because Jesus didn't say, 'I don't do crosses.' "[8]

The world will be a better place if you will do what God wants you to do. And you will be a better person, to say the least.

God has given us the example in Jesus. But here is some great news: He will enable us to follow His example. God never asks us to do something that He will not give us the strength to do, "for it is God who works in you both to will and to do for His good pleasure" (Phil. 2:13). Jesus Christ will live this life through you as you yield to Him.

CHAPTER FIVE

How to Run Well

It seems the older you get, the faster time goes. When I was in elementary school, it seemed like time moved so slowly. I remember very clearly sitting in class and watching the clock while the teacher droned on. I would think to myself, *When is this going to end? Am I going to be in elementary school for the rest of my life?* Then I went from elementary school to junior high, and time seemed to speed up a bit more. High school went a little faster.

But now instead of remembering years, I remember decades. I can even say, "I remember the twentieth century."

Someone actually figured out what time it is in your life, based on your age. For example, if you are 15, it is 10:25 in the morning of your life. If you are 20, it is 11:34 A.M. If you are 25, it is 12:42 P.M. If you are thirty, the time is 1:51 P.M. If you are 35, it is 3:00 P.M. in your life. If you are 40, it is 4:08 P.M. If you are 45, the time is 5:15 in the evening. If you are 50, it is 6:25. If you are 55, it is 7:34. If you are 60, it is 8:42. If you are 65, the time is 9:51. If you are 70, the time is 11:00 P.M. If you are older than that, you are getting close to midnight.

For me, getting older is not a depressing thought. As I look back over the years and remember the crazy hairstyles and the times when I used to actually have bad hair days, I don't wish that I were back there again. I don't wish I were 18 again or 21 again or 30. I am quite happy to be where I am at this particular moment in my life. It is a great adventure walking with Jesus Christ.

An Ongoing Effort

Maybe you are not where you were hoping you would be at this point in your spiritual life, yet I would venture to guess that you can see some dramatic improvements. As it's been said, "I am not what I can be. I am not what I should be. Thank God that I am not what I used to be."

To keep track of our progress, we need to take stock of ourselves spiritually. We should periodically ask ourselves questions such as, *Have I been growing closer to God? Has there been spiritual progress in my life? Have I developed the gifts that God has given me?*

It is a lot like cleaning house. I am the kind of person who will allow messes to build up over time. I don't like to tidy as I go. I tend to just let things go. When it gets really bad and I can no longer find things, like members of my family, then I know it is time to clean up again. In contrast to my approach, there is the way my wife Cathe cleans, which is constantly. She is always tidying and straightening things up. She will clean the dish I am still eating from. So if you take the Greg approach to cleaning house, then you will allow huge messes to build up periodically that you will clean, only to have them build up again. On the other hand, if you take the Cathe approach, you will constantly be working at it. Her approach is definitely the better one.

The same is true of our spiritual lives. We can neglect our spiritual lives to the point that messes begin to build up. They may be minor here and there, such as conflicts that need to be resolved, situations that need to be taken care of, or areas that need to be concentrated on. Or, there could be major messes for which you're now beginning to reap the consequences.

In Philippians 3, Paul gives us some principles for consistently working at our spiritual lives so we can prevent messes from building up. He talks to us about what really matters in life and what we need to be focusing on.

I think Paul must have been something of a sports fan, because he used the analogies of athletics quite often in his writing. In this passage, he compares the Christian life to running a race, and there are many principles that we can learn from this analogy.

Lose the Baggage

First, we need to get rid of all extra weight that would hinder us. Paul says,

> But whatever was to my profit I now consider loss for the sake of Christ. What is more, I consider everything a loss compared to the surpassing greatness of knowing Christ Jesus my Lord, for whose sake I have lost all things. I consider them rubbish, that I may gain Christ. (Phil. 3:7–8 NIV)

When you become a Christian, you change in so many ways. But one of the more notable changes is that you will give up many of the things you once did. Of course, it depends on what kind of lifestyle you lived prior to your conversion, but for many new believers, there will be a dramatic change that takes place.

I have heard people share their stories of how they came to Christ. They begin by talking about the great sacrifices they made to follow the Lord. Then they reflect on the life they had before Christ: "I had everything this world has to offer … I had women … I had money … We went to parties … I had so much fun. But I gave it all up for Jesus Christ!"

I find myself thinking, *What are you talking about—you gave it all up? What did you give up?* If they were to look at those things honestly and realistically, they would come to the same conclusion as Paul did: "I consider everything a loss compared to the surpassing greatness of knowing Christ Jesus." Paul was saying, "Yes, I gave up some things, but they were nothing compared to what God gave me in their place." Paul let those things go.

Some people seem to speak of their past, before they knew Christ, with more fondness than the present. That is a huge mistake. We must never glorify our past, but instead see it for what it really was: a life apart from God and a future, quite frankly, in hell. Paul knew this and said as much when speaking of his past.

If you are going to run a race, you want to run light. You don't arrive at the starting line of a marathon wearing a scuba tank, a weight belt, and fins. That would be ridiculous, because all that unnecessary equipment would hinder your progress. You run light, because you want to be equipped for the task at hand. In the same way, as we are living the Christian life, we want to cut loose any excess weight in our lives.

When I travel, I always take too much stuff with me. No matter what happens, I want to be ready for it. So, I have clothes for both warm and cold weather and anything in between. Then there are the books I like to tote along and read while traveling. Then there is my computer. The list goes on. So I end up taking way too much that I have to drag around, and I vow that the next time I will pack light. A lot of us go into the Christian life hauling excess baggage as well. We drag things along that we don't really need, things that we expend too much time and energy on or relationships that are dragging us down. It is a good idea to periodically reevaluate what we are doing and who we are doing it with and ask ourselves, "Is this a wing or a weight? This passion, pursuit, this thing that I am so interested in, is it speeding me on my way as a Christian, or is it slowing me down? Is it helping or impeding my progress?" When you are around certain people, do you find that your interest in spiritual things begins to diminish and your desire for the things of this world begins to grow? If that is the case, then it is something you need to change in your life and your friendships.

As we run this race, we should run to receive the prize.

Paul wrote to Timothy, "Flee also youthful lusts; but pursue righteousness, faith, love, peace with those who call on the Lord out of a pure heart" (2 Timothy 2:22). Running the race is not just running to what is right. It is also running away from what is wrong. And it is also running with others who are like-minded.

We read in Hebrews 12:2, "Therefore we also, since we are surrounded by so great a cloud of witnesses, let us lay aside every weight, and the sin which so easily ensnares us, and let us run with endurance the race that is set before us." A distinction is made here between sin and a weight. If you want to know what sin is, just read the Bible. I would suggest starting with the Ten Commandments. Sin is sin, and it is the same for every person.

But then there are weights. Something that would potentially slow you down would not necessarily slow me down, because we are different. Or it might slow me down, but it would not necessarily slow you down.

It is like having different metabolisms. I had a very fast metabolism for many years. I would eat fattening food anytime day or night and never put on an ounce. I was as slim as slim could be. Then when I hit my 30s, I had to say goodbye to my foolish ways.

I have a friend who has a super-fast metabolism. No matter what he eats, he never seems to gain weight. When he was younger, I would warn him, "Your metabolism is going to change. When you hit your 30s, you will start putting on weight." He hit his 30s and nothing happened. So I said, "When you are 40, it is going to happen." Now he is in his 50s, and he is still as skinny as a rail. He still eats everything in sight and never puts on an ounce. Meanwhile, I can just look at a few dinner rolls and gain four pounds. We have different metabolisms.

So we need to look at things in our lives and ask, "Is this a weight for me?" Just because one Christian can do something does not necessarily mean you should, especially if you have an uneasy conscience about it. The Bible says, "Whatever is not from faith is sin" (Rom. 14:23). Or as another translation says, "Whatever is done without a conviction of its approval by God is sinful" (AMP). One paraphrase of this verse says, "But anyone who believes that something he wants to do is wrong shouldn't do it. He sins if he does, for he thinks it is wrong, and so for him, it is wrong" (TLB). We might protest and say, "But so-and-so is doing it!" But you are not that person. You must be obedient to what He tells you to do. Some are weaker than others in some areas. Therefore, what may be the potential downfall for one may not necessarily be the same for someone else.

Play by the Rules or Be Disqualified

Second, we must play by the rules, or we will be disqualified. Paul said, "I discipline my body like an athlete, training it to do what it should. Otherwise, I fear that after preaching to others I myself might be disqualified" (1 Cor. 9:27 NLT). We have all seen the consequences of Olympic athletes breaking the rules or even slightly bending them. They are disqualified, regardless of how well they have done in their particular athletic event.

As we are running the race of life, as we are walking with God, we need to play by His rules. This means that we don't make up the rules as we go or bend the rules or disregard the rules. We understand that God has put parameters in place for our own good. When the Bible teaches us that certain things are wrong, we should go out of our way to avoid them. And when it teaches us that certain things are right, we should go out of our way to embrace them and do them.

Run with the Right Motive

Third, we must run with the right motive. Paul tells us as we run this race, we should run to receive the prize: "Don't you realize that in a race everyone runs, but only one person gets the prize? So run to win! All athletes are disciplined in their training. They do it to win a prize that will fade away, but we do it for an eternal prize" (1 Cor. 9:24–25 NLT).

Athletes who compete in the Olympics compete for the gold medal. They don't get their picture on the Wheaties box if they win the bronze, as commendable as that is. Frankly, I would be overjoyed to earn such an honor as the bronze. I would be thrilled to even compete in the Olympics. But everyone hopes for that gold medal.

Silver is great, too, but the gold is what the athletes want. That is where the prestige is. That is where the endorsements are.

Paul says we have to run for the prize. As I am running this race, I know there is a reward in heaven waiting for me one day, based on how faithful I am to what God has called me to do. The same is true for you as a follower of Jesus Christ, living this same way.

Keep Your Eyes on Jesus

Fourth, we must always keep our eyes firmly fixed on Jesus. Hebrews 12:2 tells us we run this race by "keeping our eyes on Jesus, the champion who initiates and perfects our faith. Because of the joy awaiting him, he endured the cross, disregarding its shame. Now he is seated in the place of honor beside God's throne" (NLT). Jesus is the one whom we all should be running for.

This is why Paul was running. His purpose, what mattered to him, was to know Jesus Christ: "That I may know Him and the power of His resurrection, and the fellowship of His sufferings, being conformed to His death" (Phil. 3:10).

When I was in high school, I was a pretty decent runner. And when I used to run, I always ran a bit faster when there was a crowd watching. Practicing wasn't as fun, because no one was there to impress. But if one pretty girl showed up, I started running well.

We have an even better motivation than I did back in high school. We have the Lord Jesus himself watching us.

Beware of Those Who Want to Stop You

Fifth, we must beware of those who want to stop us from running this race. Paul wrote to the churches of Galatia, "You were running a good race. Who cut in on you and kept you from obeying the truth? That kind of persuasion does not come from the one who calls you" (Gal. 5:7–8 NIV).

Paul was focused. He said, "Brethren, I do not count myself to have apprehended; but *one thing I do*, forgetting those things which are behind and reaching forward to those things which are ahead" (Phil. 3:13, emphasis mine).

David had this focus as well. He wrote, "*One thing* I have desired of the Lord, that will I seek: that I may dwell in the house of the Lord all the days of my life, to behold the beauty of the Lord, and to inquire in His temple" (Ps. 27:4, emphasis mine). Here was a man who was going through life saying that the one thing that really excites him is spending time in the presence of God.

Mary knew this one thing, too, when Jesus came to visit her, her sister Martha, and their brother Lazarus at their home in Bethany. She sat down at His feet because she saw a tremendous opportunity to hear what Jesus had to say. Martha, a hardworking woman, wanted to impress the Lord with a fine meal. And that is understandable if you had a guest like Jesus.

So as Martha was working away, she kept looking for Mary. Finally, in frustration, she walked in, probably covered with food, and basically said, "Lord, would You tell my sister to get in here and help me?" But Jesus told her, "You are worried and upset about many things, but only *one thing* is needed. Mary has chosen what is better, and it will not be taken away from her" (Luke 10:41–42 NIV, emphasis mine). In other words, "Martha, I appreciate all of your hard work. But Mary figured out one thing here, and that is to sit at My feet."

This is what Paul was saying: This one thing I do. ... He had focus in life. He knew where he was going. He knew his purpose for running. "Looking unto Jesus"—that is what will keep us moving forward in the race of life.

There are things that will discourage us in this race. People will discourage us. Circumstances will discourage us. The devil will discourage us. But just keep your sights on the Lord, and keep moving forward.

The best way to move a tired horse in the right direction is to turn her toward home. If you have ever ridden a stable horse, then you know the horse won't obey when you are leaving the stables. In fact, she won't do anything you say. But when you turn that horse back toward the barn, suddenly she obeys—or she moves in that direction at least.

If you want to get your life moving in the right direction, then focus it on God and move in that direction. There are so many things that can distract us from this race and so many things we can chase after. Matthew 6:33 tells us, "But seek first the kingdom of God and His righteousness, and all these things shall be added to you." In the context of that statement, Jesus was talking about unbelievers who only think about what they are going to wear, eat, or drink. He was saying, "Don't sweat this stuff. Focus on the kingdom of God. Put God's Word and His principles at the forefront of your life, and your Heavenly Father will take care of these other things."

It is that "one thing." The main thing is to keep the main thing the main thing. The main thing is following

Jesus and the plan that He has for your life. That is what Paul was saying: "This one thing I do. I am not going to let anyone or anything draw me from this." Is that what you are doing right now?

Don't Look Back

Sixth, to run this race effectively, we cannot look back. Paul said, "Forgetting those things which are behind and reaching forward to those things which are ahead, I press toward the goal for the prize of the upward call of God in Christ Jesus" (Phil. 3:13–14). In the original language, "forgetting" does not mean "failing to remember." It means to no longer be influenced or affected by something.

Everyone who has ever run a race knows that you can break your stride by looking over your shoulder to see how your opponent is doing. More than once, a runner who was in the lead lost the race by looking back. When you run, when you see that finish line, you are supposed to throw your head back, push your chest out, and give it everything you have. Sometimes it is mere inches separating one runner from another.

We have to stay focused. We have to go forward.

When God said, "I, even I, am He who blots out your transgressions for My own sake; and I will not remember your sins" (Isa. 43:25), He was not suggesting that He will have lapses in memory. Rather, He was saying that He will no longer hold your sin against you. That sin can no longer affect your standing with Him or influence His attitude toward you.

Therefore, we need to do what God does: forget our past. We should not choose to remember what God has chosen to forget. Sometimes we will dredge up things that we did wrong. We will go over it again and again in our minds. Meanwhile, God is in effect saying, "I have forgotten all about that. Why have you brought it up? Forget about it. " One sure way to forget your past is to not repeat your mistakes. It is not so serious to make a mistake as it is to repeat it. If you learn a lesson from burning your fingers and don't do it again, then that is a well-learned lesson. It's called failing forward. We need to learn from our mistakes and remember some of the bitter lessons we have learned. But we no longer need to be controlled by our past. This is what Paul meant by using this word "forgetting."

Consider the fact that Paul had done some horrible things. He was responsible for the death of Stephen and perhaps other Christian men and women and had to carry that in his conscience until his final day. But he was able to put his past in the past and accept the forgiveness of God.

Maybe you have done some horrible things as well. But to effectively forget, you must first be forgiven. And this forgiveness will only come when you ask God for it. The Bible says, "If we confess our sins, He is faithful and just to forgive us our sins and to cleanse us from all unrighteousness" (1 John 1:9).

Do you have any sin you need to confess and turn from today? Are you still dragging around the guilt of some wrong things you have done? You can be completely forgiven. You can end this day with your slate wiped clean by Jesus Christ. You can say with Paul, "Forgetting those things which are behind and reaching forward to those things which are ahead, I press toward the goal. ..." This is something you need to do if you are going to run in the race of life.

But there is something else we need to forget: we need to forget our victories. I don't mean that we cannot look back on our lives and give thanks for the Lord's faithfulness, because that is a very good thing to do. I mean that we are not to live in the past. Some people live in a spiritual time warp. All they want to talk about is what God did thirty years ago. But that was then and this is now. Tomorrow is another day with new opportunities. We need to press on and move forward to what God has ahead.

Cross the Finish Line

Last, we must finish the race we have begun. Once we begin running, we need to keep moving.

Have you ever been in a race where your body was wracked with pain? Your lungs are burning. Your muscles are throbbing. Your legs feel like rubber flopping around. But there is the finish line right before you. There is the ribbon. You know you have to finish the race.

Paul was saying, "Don't let anyone or anything stop you." It takes determination to follow Christ. It is not easy. You will be harassed. You will be laughed at. You will be mocked. You might even be killed.

Maybe you have been running this race, but you have been slowing down a little. You've thought, *I am a little winded. I am getting on in years. I think that I have run so well for so long that I am going to slow down now. I am going to sit down here for a couple of years.*

But if you run in first place for nine-tenths of the race and then bail out at the end, it doesn't count.

Paul candidly admitted that he had not reached a

spiritual plateau: "I don't mean to say that I have already achieved these things or that I have already reached perfection. But I press on to possess that perfection for which Christ Jesus first possessed me" (Phil. 3:12 NLT). He was saying, "I have so far to go." Paul had led countless people to faith. He had established churches. He had written epistles. If anyone could boast, it was Paul. Yet he did not boast. He said he had so much to learn and so far to go. Paul was saying that he couldn't live off his experiences. He needed to keep moving forward.

A sign along an airport runway says, "Keep moving. If you stop, you are in danger and a danger to those who are flying." The same is true for us. We always need to keep growing spiritually and keep moving forward as Christians. If we stop, we are in danger and a danger to those around us. We cannot afford to rest on our laurels.

This race we are running is a long-distance run. It doesn't matter whether you have held first position for nine-tenths of the race. If you stop short of the finish line, you won't win. You have to cross that line.

My wife is very good at cycling. She can ride long distances. But when I started riding with her, I had to learn the importance of pacing. On one of my first long-distance rides, I wasn't enjoying it much at the beginning. But then my muscles began to warm up, and after awhile, I began passing everyone. But then I didn't have any energy left to finish the ride. Someone had to push me part of the way. That is because I didn't pace myself. And let me tell you, it is very humiliating to be pushed on a bicycle.

The Christian life can be like that. When you begin, it is such a new and different life. Some don't make it. Some back out. Still others say, "I am going for it." They make it through the first few difficulties and start growing spiritually. Then they start getting bursts of energy. But the key is to pace ourselves to finish the race and make it across the finish line.

I don't know where you are in your Christian life right now. If you are young, then you may think you have many years to get this all worked out. Maybe you do and maybe you don't. Only God knows. That is why you want to run every lap as though it were your last. Make it all count. Give it your best. You have to press on. You have to finish the race you started.

During a military campaign, a young captain was recommended to Napoleon for promotion to higher rank. Napoleon asked, "Why do you suggest this man in particular?" It was explained that because of the captain's unusual courage on the battlefield a few days earlier, a victory had been won. "Very good," Napoleon replied, "but what did he do the next day?"

I think God would ask the same thing of us. The Christian life is a daily experience. It is not Sunday to Sunday; it is 24/7. We continue on in the things of God. We don't take days off from discipleship. We don't take spiritual vacations. The Bible says that His mercies are new every morning (see Lam. 3:22–23).

Let's not live in the past. Let's move forward as believers. The days have never been darker. At the same time, opportunities have never been greater. This is a race that you must run. Look at your life. If you need to make any changes, do it today. You can begin tomorrow on the right foot with your priorities in order and your focus clear.

CHAPTER SIX

No Worries!

Polls in recent years have shown that the anxiety level of Americans is almost as high as it was in the immediate aftermath of 9/11. A Gallup poll found that 69 percent of the respondents said heightened terrorist alerts has caused additional concern. Worry and anxiety are at an all-time high in America today.

A lot of things can make a person afraid today. With the war in Iraq, threats of terrorism, the threat of an economic recession, and a presidential election approaching, there is reason to be concerned. But worrying is not a productive thing to do, because it is a failure to trust God. Not only that, but it stirs up your own anxiety. The word "worry" comes from an old German word meaning "to strangle or choke." And that is exactly what worry will do. It will create a mental and emotional stranglehold on your life. It does not make things better. In fact, for all practical purposes, it makes them worse. When you worry about the future, you cripple yourself in the present.

Every day has its own quota of problems. Some of them are constant from day to day. Others come and go. But when you get up in the morning, whatever challenges, adversities, or difficulties you are going to be facing are your quota for the day. So why go after tomorrow's quota as well? Why start worrying about things that haven't even started yet? When you do that, you actually hurt yourself, because worrying does not empty tomorrow of its sorrow; it empties today of its strength.

Jesus said, "Therefore do not worry about tomorrow, for tomorrow will worry about itself. Each day has enough trouble of its own" (Matthew 6:34 NIV). God will give you the strength to face each and every day with enough grace to manage. His grace is sufficient for us. He is the same yesterday, today, and forever. He will not abandon you in your hour of need. But if you worry, you will only compound your troubles.

A story is told about a man who came face-to-face with the dangers of worry. One morning, he saw Death walking toward his town. The man stopped Death and asked, "What are you going to do?"

Death said, "I am going to take one hundred people."

The man hurried ahead of Death into the town to warn everyone of what Death was planning to do.

As evening fell, he met Death again. The man said, "You told me you were going to take one hundred people. So why did one thousand die?"

"I kept my word," Death told him. "I took only one hundred people. Worry took the rest."

Studies have shown that many physical illnesses can actually be brought on by worry and anxiety. Many of the people in hospital beds in the United States today are constant worriers. Forty-three percent of all adults suffer health effects due to worry and stress. And 79 to 90 percent of all visits to primary care physicians are stress-related complaints or disorders. We are a nation filled with anxiety and worry.

When you add this to the challenges we are facing collectively in this country, it only makes matters worse. This epitaph could be written on countless American gravestones: "Hurried, worried, buried.

Australians have an expression they use quite frequently. If you ask for directions or place an order in a restaurant, they will answer and then often add, "No worries, mate." Not only is it pleasant, but it is theologically sound.

Most of the things we worry about never happen anyway. One survey on worry revealed that only 8 percent of what people worried about were legitimate matters of concern, while the other 92 percent were imaginary. In other words, what people worried about never happened or was beyond their control.

Worry doesn't help. It only hurts. I am not saying we should not be concerned or aware or take practical steps to prevent things from happening. What I am saying is that worry itself is not productive.

Philippians 4 provides some practical information about what we should do instead of worrying. These principles, if applied, will give us victory over worry. It is significant to realize that when Paul wrote these words, he was in a very troubling situation. It had been Paul's desire to go to Rome and preach when he was arrested and put into prison, a dark dungeon with no ventilation. As he wrote his epistle to the Philippians, he was awaiting his fate. It was a pathetic, miserable situation in which he found himself.

Paul was facing uncertainty, yet he was not worried. He had great peace. And he tells us how to have victory over worry: "Rejoice in the Lord always. Again I will say, rejoice!" (v. 4). In the original language, this is not a suggestion, but a command. In other words, God is commanding us to rejoice. To disobey this is to disobey God.

We try and justify our worry by saying, "You don't understand. This is so difficult." I know it is difficult. Paul didn't say, "Rejoice in your circumstances." He said, "Rejoice in the Lord." Despite what you are going through, remember that God is still on the throne. He still loves you. His plans for you are still good. He said, "I will never leave you nor forsake you" (Hebrews 13:5).

Right Praying

Winning over worry begins with right praying. Paul follows his admonition to rejoice with an important principle for prayer: "Be anxious for nothing, but in everything by prayer and supplication, with thanksgiving, let your requests be made known to God" (v. 6). Notice the words "in everything by prayer." Paul didn't say, "in some things by prayer" or "only the really big things by prayer." Rather, he said, "In everything by prayer and supplication, with thanksgiving, let your requests be made known to God." This reminds us that nothing is too big or too small to bring to God in prayer. He is interested in even the smallest of details.

Paul was saying, "Don't worry about these things, but rather pray about them." The next time you are tempted to worry, pray instead. We need to get into the habit of turning to God when we feel worry approaching so that our reaction in times of trouble will be like a conditioned reflex.

A normal reflex is not taught; it is automatic. If I reach out and touch a hot iron, I pull my hand back. I didn't have to teach myself to do that, because I will automatically pull away from something that causes pain. Even an infant would pull his or her hand away from something hot. It is an automatic reflex.

Then there is a conditioned reflex. When you're at an event and hear the Star Spangled Banner begin to play, you stand up. That is a conditioned reflex. You know that you are to stand up in honor of our national anthem.

When you were learning to drive, you had to consciously think about everything you did. You would plan to hit the brake as you were approaching a stoplight. You would plan to signal your turn. Now when you drive, you no longer think about each and every action. That is because you've trained yourself and have developed a conditioned reflex.

Our natural tendency when we're troubled is not necessarily to pray. In many cases, our natural tendency is to embrace worry: *What if this happens? What about that?* Then you come up with more things to worry about, and suddenly you are feeling completely overwhelmed.

But if we can develop a conditioned reflex during troubling times, our automatic response will be to pray. We intentionally place the matter in God's hands. As someone wisely said, "When your knees start knocking, kneel on them."

Often when we face adversity, our first instinct is to turn to people for help. There is indeed a time for turning to people, but people should not be the primary place we turn. We must teach ourselves to turn to God.

As we do so, we don't want to neglect an important element of prayer: thanksgiving. Verse 6 says, "In everything by prayer and supplication, *with thanksgiving*, let your requests be made known to God" (emphasis mine). As we take time to worship our heavenly Father, reminding ourselves of His greatness and power, we automatically put our problems into their proper perspective. As we contemplate the greatness and awesomeness of God, we see our problems in their corresponding smallness.

This is why Jesus taught us to pray, "Our Father in heaven, hallowed be Your name. Your kingdom come. Your will be done on earth as it is in heaven. Give us day by day our daily bread" (Luke 11:2–3). Our inclination would be to cut to the chase: "Our Father in heaven, give us day by day our daily bread." But Jesus essentially was saying, "Before you offer a word of personal petition, say, 'Father, You are in heaven. You are powerful. You are to be revered and worshiped.' " Before we utter a word regarding our own needs, we should recognize who God is and submit to His will for our lives, whatever it may be. That puts everything into perspective.

Have you prayed about your problems? Have you been praying about the thing that is troubling you, that has been tormenting you?

Paul was not saying that we would always receive the things we ask for. But he was saying that no matter what, God will give us peace in the midst of our storms. We need to trust in the providence of God.

The next verse covers two places where worry originates: "And the peace of God, which surpasses all understanding, will guard your *hearts* and *minds* through Christ Jesus" (v. 7, emphasis mine). The heart is the source of wrong feelings, and the mind is the source of wrong thinking. Paul was saying that God's peace will guard them. Paul was using a military term, saying that God's peace literally will stand guard around your heart and protect you if, in everything by prayer and supplication, with thanksgiving, you let your requests be made known to God.

We see an example of this in Daniel, who prayed every day. The Bible tells us he would open his windows, get down on his knees, and call out to God. Daniel had some enemies who wanted him destroyed, because he had found favor with the king. Yet when they looked for scandal in his life, they could find none. Eventually they convinced the king to authorize a law that prevented his subjects from praying to anyone but him. Anyone who disobeyed the law would be thrown into a den of lions.

Now if you were Daniel, what would you have done? You might have thought, *I think God would understand if I closed my windows for my prayer meetings.* Sometimes as Christians we are embarrassed to pray in public. But Daniel wasn't embarrassed. He wasn't about to hide. He would pray as he always did. And sure enough, he was arrested and thrown into the den of lions. There was nothing the king could do, because he had signed his own decree and could not change it. So Daniel spent the night in the lion's den. Guess who slept like a baby? Daniel. Guess who was up all night? The king.

When you worry about the future, you cripple yourself in the present.

Daniel probably saw it as a win-win situation. Option 1: He would get a good night's sleep, using the big old cats for soft pillows. Option 2: He would be the lions' dinner and would wake up in heaven. Either way, he was OK.

Of course, we know that God preserved Daniel's life, and Daniel explained to the king that God had shut the lions' mouths. It is a classic story of answered prayer.

But there is another important lesson we can learn from Daniel's story. He prayed and gave thanks to God, even after he found out that he could be arrested for it (see Dan. 6:10). Daniel did exactly what Paul was telling us to do here in Philippians 4. He prayed and gave thanks.

As 1 Peter 5:7 says, "Cast all your anxiety on him because he cares for you" (NIV). Two words jump out from this verse: "cast" and "care." The word "cast" is not the term we use for throwing something. Rather, it signifies a definite act of the will by which we stop worrying about things and let God assume the responsibility for our welfare. The word "care" means that God is mindful of your interests. He is concerned about you. If it bothers you, then it is of concern to Him. If it is troubling you, then He wants to intervene and help you.

The psalmist wrote, "How precious also are Your thoughts to me, O God! How great is the sum of them!" (Ps. 139:17) and "I am poor and needy; yet the Lord thinks upon me" (Ps. 40:17). Let it be a great comfort to know that God is thinking about you right now. You can cast all your cares on Him, knowing He cares for you.

Right Thinking

In addition to right praying, winning over worry requires right thinking:

> Finally, brethren, whatever things are true, whatever things are noble, whatever things are just, whatever things are pure, whatever things are lovely, whatever things are of good report, if there is any virtue and if there is anything praiseworthy—meditate on these things. (v. 8)

Maintaining personal peace involves both the heart and the mind. Isaiah 26:3 says, "You will keep him in perfect peace, whose mind is stayed on You, because he trusts in You." We must think properly about things.

What we think about ultimately affects what we do. Therefore, you must nip in the bud any thoughts that are impure, spiritually harmful, or that feed the beast of worry. This means refusing to play the what-if game, driving yourself to despair. Train your mind to think properly and biblically. We read in 2 Corinthians 10:5 that we should cast down "arguments and every high thing that exalts itself against the knowledge of God, bringing every thought into captivity to the obedience of Christ." Fill your mind with the things of God.

The next time you are troubled, try talking to yourself. Why? Because we need to train our minds to think biblically and rein in our emotions accordingly. Faith does not begin working automatically. We must first apply it. For example, we read in Psalm 42 that the psalmist was troubled. His emotions seemed to be getting the best of him, causing him to cry out, "Why are you downcast, O my soul? Why so disturbed within me?" (v. 15 NIV). Then he talked to himself. In other words, he applied faith, reason, and biblical thinking to the situation. He said, "Put your hope in God, for I will yet praise him, my Savior and my God" (vv. 5–6 NIV).

The next time you're struggling with doubt or temptation, talk to yourself. Quote Scripture to yourself. Remind yourself of what is true. Remind yourself of your faith. Every believer needs to do this, regardless of how many years he or she has been a Christian. You can have a lapse of faith. You can have a moment of despair. You can have a time in which you don't understand what is going on in your life. It happens to the best of them. Even a great man of faith like Abraham had his moments of doubt.

Right thinking means refusing to think about troubling things. It means remaining resolute, even when the devil attacks. It means saying, "I refuse to be worried. I have done the right thing. I have done what I believe to be right and legitimate. I will wait on God, and I refuse to worry about this."

Some people suggest that following Jesus Christ means no longer thinking clearly, in a reasonable manner. But nothing could be further from the truth.

I find it interesting that the way God chose to give His revelation to humanity was in a book, in the written word. He didn't give it to us in a picture or a painting. He didn't give it to us in a movie. He didn't give it to us in a music video or a song. He gave it to us in writing. Why? So we would think, read, and reason.

The most clear-thinking person on Earth today is the biblically literate Christian who looks at things in a logical and reasonable matter. God said, "Come now, and let us reason together …" (Isa. 1:18). Christians can put into context what is going on in the world. We understand that humanity is not inherently good. We understand that the source of our problems is sin. We understand that technology never will solve our problems, and neither will politics or any human solution. We understand that the only real solution is the intervention of God. We understand that the way for people to change is through an encounter with Jesus Christ.

Even in the midst of turmoil, a Christian can have the peace that passes all human understanding. I have witnessed it. I have talked with believers who are terminally ill or who are facing the most adverse of circumstances, and I have seen that peace in action. Only Christ can give that. The world can't give it. Alcohol can't give it. A drug can't give it. Only God can.

Right Living

Last, winning over worry requires right living. Paul wrote to the believers at Philippi, "The things which you learned and received and heard and saw in me, these do, and the God of peace will be with you" (v. 9). You can't separate outward action from inward attitude. The way you think determines the way you live. So if you are engaged in right praying and thinking, then you will be engaged in right living.

Sin, on the other hand, always results in turmoil and unrest. Isaiah 57:20 describes the unbeliever this way: "But the wicked are like the troubled sea, when it cannot rest, whose waters cast up mire and dirt. 'There is no peace,' says my God, 'for the wicked.' "

As we live in purity as Christians, we will experience God's peace: "The work of righteousness will be peace, and the effect of righteousness, quietness and assurance forever" (Isa. 32:17).

Do you have the peace that passes all human understanding right now? Or is your life in turmoil and upheaval because you are searching for answers and gripped with anxiety, panic, and worry? There is a solution.

However, what I have been writing about in this chapter applies to Christians only. You can pray all you want, but until you know God, your prayers won't go much higher than the ceiling. The only real prayer that God hears from an unbeliever is: "God, be merciful to me a sinner. ... Lord, forgive me." Before you can have the peace of God, you must first have peace with God.

Until you have asked Jesus to come into your life and be your Savior and Lord, until you have turned from your sin, then you are in a war with God. And you are going to lose that war. It's only a matter of time.

But God loves you. God wants to forgive you. God wants you to enter into a relationship with Him. Just call on Him and find this peace. If you have not yet given your life to Jesus Christ, do it today. In the back of this book, I've explained step-by-step how you can do that.

Whatever you might be facing, you don't have to face it alone. God can help you. As you apply the principles of right praying, right thinking, and right living, you can win over worry.

CHAPTER SEVEN

The Picture of Contentment

A wealthy employer was walking through his office one day and overheard one of his employees say, "If only I had $1,000, then I would be perfectly content."

So he walked over to the employee and said, "I overheard what you were saying. I want to help you out. I am going to write you a check for $1,000, because I have never met a perfectly content person." Then he took out his checkbook, wrote out a check for $1,000, tore it out, and gave it to the employee.

As he was walking away, he overheard the employee say to her coworker, "I should have asked for $2,000."

Would you describe yourself as content? Are you happy with what you have and where you are right now? Or would you be content if only you were a little bit smarter or a little bit better-looking or had a little more money?

In Philippians 4, we have been given the picture of a perfectly contented man: Paul. As we examine this picture, we will find the secret of contentment.

While one of the major themes of this epistle is joy, it is worth noting that Paul was facing some very difficult circumstances personally. We know that he was a Roman prisoner, and his trial was approaching. He didn't know whether he would be acquitted or put to death. Chained to a Roman guard, he was unable to go out and preach the gospel, which for Paul was almost a fate worse than death.

In the midst of these difficult circumstances, Paul reminds us of the importance of rejoicing and tells us that we can have joy in the Lord.

It's All in the Mind

So what was the secret of Paul's joy and contentment? The answer to that question is found in a word that is often used by Paul in this epistle: "mind." Paul uses it ten times and the word "think" five times. Add to this the number of times he uses "remember," and you have a total of sixteen references to the mind. In other words, Paul is saying that the secret of joy and contentment is found in the way a believer thinks. It is his or her attitude, or outlook.

Paul was not teaching positive thinking or possibility thinking. Nor was he offering shallow self-help principles. This was a man who had been in the nitty-gritty of life. He was saying, "Here is how I have learned to have joy and contentment in a troubled world: it is all in the way that you think. It is the way that you perceive things. It is your attitude."

We have seen these principles throughout Philippians. Paul was single-minded. He knew what really mattered in life. He understood that the main thing was to keep the main thing the main thing. He knew where he was going in life and had his priorities in order. And first and foremost in his life was Jesus Christ.

Paul had the mind of Christ, which is the mind of a servant—the mind of a person who puts the needs of others above his own.

He also had the mind of spiritual growth and progression. Paul was not one to rest on his laurels or to believe that he had reached a state of spiritual perfection or a plateau of some kind. He knew there was still far to go: "Not that I have already attained, or am already perfected; but I press on, that I may lay hold of that for which Christ Jesus has also laid hold of me" (Phil. 3:12).

Last, Paul had a rejoicing mind. He reminded the Philippians to "rejoice in the Lord always. Again I will say, rejoice!" (Phil. 4:4).

It's Whom You Know

Now, as he draws his epistle to a close, Paul reveals the secret of contentment:

> But I rejoiced in the Lord greatly that now at last your care for me has flourished again; though you surely did care, but you lacked opportunity. Not that I speak in regard to need, for I have learned in whatever state I am, to be content: I know how to be abased, and I know how to abound. Everywhere and in all things I have learned both to be full and to be hungry, both to abound and to suffer need. I can do all things through Christ who strengthens me. (Phil. 4:10–13)

We think contentment comes from what we have: *If I just had $1,000 … If I were a little more successful … If I were just married … Or, If I were just married to a different person … If I had more ministry opportunities …* It is a never-ending pursuit of something that is always just beyond our grasp. But Paul said, "I have learned in whatever state I am, to be content." Remember, he was in prison when he made that statement. Paul was not offering this belief as a mere classroom theory. It came from the school of life. He had experienced pain and pleasure, health and sickness, weakness and strength, wealth and poverty. He was a hero to some and a villain to others. But he was someone who had found complete contentment.

Note Paul's use of the word "learned": "I have learned in whatever state I am, to be content." This is actually a word generally used by the pagans of his day to describe some special attainment or initiation into some hidden truth. So Paul was saying, "Check this out. I have been 'initiated.' I have found the hidden truth. I have found the secret of contentment." There is clearly a note of satire in his words, yet he was making this poignant truth.

The word Paul used for "content" is also important. It is a word that means "self-sufficient." In the context of this epistle, it is speaking of a sufficiency in Jesus Christ. Paul was flexible. He was saying, "I can be in a palace and be content, or I can be at the bottom of the bottom and be content. It is all about my relationship with God."

It is God who is working, but we must be yielding.

Contentment isn't based on what we have; it is based on whom we know. Hebrews 13:5 tells us, "Let your conduct be without covetousness; be content with such things as you have. For He Himself has said, 'I will never leave you nor forsake you.' " In the original language, this statement could be translated, "I will never, no never, no never leave you or forsake you." He will be with you no matter what you face in life. That is a great assurance. Find your contentment there.

As David said, "The Lord is my shepherd; I shall not

want" (Ps. 23:1). If you are always in want, then maybe the Lord is not yet your Shepherd. If He really is your Shepherd, then you will find satisfaction and fulfillment in Him, whether He blesses you with a little or much. That is how Paul could say, "I can do all things through Christ who strengthens me" (v. 13). His contentment came as a result of his close and intimate fellowship with Jesus, which allowed him to be lifted above his circumstances and gave him the strength to deal with whatever came his way.

Do Your Part

Not only that, but Paul's statement shows us our part and God's part. Paul did not say that the Christian should do everything for himself or herself. Nor did he say that God will do everything for the Christian. It shows us that God will do certain things, and we must then respond. God's power and resources are there, but we must appropriate them. So instead of saying, "Christ does everything and I do nothing," Paul said, "I can do all things through Christ who strengthens me." God has given us the strength to be the people He has called us to be, but we must appropriate, apply, and use that strength.

There are some things that only God can do and some things that only we can do. Only God can enable, but only we can yield. Only God can guide, but only we can follow. Only God can convict us of our sin, but only we can repent of it. God will not step over the boundary of our free will and make us do what He wants. If He did, then we would be mere robots. But because He wants us to act out of our own free will, He initiates, and then we must respond to what He is doing.

It is the same principle behind Paul's exhortation to "work out your own salvation with fear and trembling; for it is God who works in you both to will and to do for His good pleasure" (Phil. 2:12–13). Another way to translate this would be, "Carry to the goal and fully complete your salvation with self-distrust, for it is God who works in you." So we see that it is God who is working, but we must be yielding.

Many times we are not taking hold of the resources God has given to us. In our own strength, we try to effectively resist temptation or witness more boldly for Christ or be a better husband or wife. As a result, we fall short. Jesus said, "Without Me you can do nothing" (John 15:5). Here is the choice in life: You can go in your own strength and try to make it happen and fail. Or you can say, "I can't do it, Lord, but I can do all things through Christ who strengthens me. I am yielding to the power of the Holy Spirit. I am taking steps of practical obedience." And everything can turn around.

The Joy of Giving

Of course, we can talk all day about walking with God and being strengthened by Him, but if it does not affect the way we live, and specifically, the way we give, it means nothing. There is perhaps no clearer evidence of spiritual maturity than financial generosity. Martin Luther said there are three conversions necessary: the conversion of the heart, the conversion of the mind, and the conversion of the pocketbook. This is often the last area we will turn over to God. We want to retain complete control. We are uncomfortable when the topic is even brought up. But it may be that our discomfort is an indicator that this area is not in its proper order in our lives.

The Bible addresses the topic quite frequently. It is the main focus of nearly half the parables Jesus told. In addition, one in every seven verses in the New Testament deals with the subject of money. To give you an idea of how that compares with other topics, the Bible offers about five hundred verses on prayer, less than five hundred verses about faith, and two thousand verses about money.

Paul approaches the subject in verse 18 as well: "Indeed I have all and abound. I am full, having received from Epaphroditus the things sent from you, a sweet-smelling aroma, an acceptable sacrifice, well pleasing to God" (v. 18). Epaphroditus had brought a special offering to Paul from the believers in Philippi. This deeply touched the apostle, because these believers were giving sacrificially and cheerfully when others who were even more able were not giving at all. Paul commended them for their generosity, letting these believers know that their giving was a sweet-smelling aroma to God.

Principles for Giving

God wants this area to be in balance in our lives as well, and 1 Corinthians 16 gives us insight into how we as believers are to give:

> Now concerning the collection for the saints, as I have given orders to the churches of Galatia, so you must do also: On the first day of the week let each one of you lay something aside, storing up as he may prosper, that there be no collections when I come. And when

I come, whomever you approve by your letters I will send to bear your gift to Jerusalem. (vv. 1–16)

These verses help us understand what the Bible teaches about giving. First, we see that giving is a universal practice: "As I have given orders to the churches of Galatia, so you must do also" (v. 1). In other words, every church should give. As a result, every individual Christian should give.

Second, we see that it was done to be done every week: "On the first day of the week … lay something aside …" (v. 2). This is one of the first indications, by the way, that the early Christians had begun to gather on a regular basis on Sunday for worship, prayer, Bible study, and giving.

Third, we see that giving is a personal act: "Let each one of you lay something aside …" (v. 2). Paul was saying that each of them should give. He wasn't leaving anyone out. I believe we need to teach our kids the importance of giving. Even if they put just a few coins into the offering, it teaches them the principle of giving to God.

Hopefully we set something aside to give because we want to and because we recognize the blessing that comes from doing it. We don't do it out of pressure or constraint, because the Bible clearly teaches that God loves a cheerful giver (see 2 Cor. 9:7).

"Why give? What's in it for me?" are not the right questions to ask, but let me address them anyway. There is something in it for us when we give: "Not that I seek the gift," Paul said, "but I seek the fruit that abounds to your account" (Phil 4:17). How important it is for us to realize that when we invest in the work of the kingdom, it is an investment that pays spiritual dividends. One of the ways to be a part of what God is doing in the world is to give to the work of His kingdom. This means setting aside a percentage our income each and every month for this purpose. That is not legalism; it is good planning and obedience for a life that is dedicated to God.

Most churches today are supported financially by a relatively small percentage of believers who give their tithes and offerings on a weekly basis. Some Christians will give sporadically at best and at worst, not give at all. But there is a core of people who understand what the Bible teaches about giving and faithfully engage. Because of their faithfulness, they make it possible for others to be on the receiving end of ministry. They have discovered the joy of giving, and I would even venture to say that as a result, they have discovered the secret of contentment.

The Conditions of God's Provision

Some may say, "I am lacking in finances. How can I give? I can't afford to give." Personally, I can't afford *not* to give, because I want to be a part of what God is doing. This brings us to a verse that is often misinterpreted and misapplied: "And my God shall supply all your need according to His riches in glory by Christ Jesus" (v. 19). Here Paul was writing to the believers about their faithful and sacrificial gift to him. They didn't give frivolously; they gave with the right motive. The need Paul was referring to came about because of their sacrificial gift. It was not created by poor stewardship, unwillingness to work, laziness, extravagance, or foolish spending.

Most financial problems are a result of one of these things, but this is not why the believers at Philippi were in need. They had a need because they gave sacrificially to

Paul. Paul was saying to them that God would
supply all their need according to His riches in Christ
Jesus. In other words, "Because you have given with the
right motive, because your life is in balance, because you
have your priorities in order, God will take care of you."

However, this verse does not say that God will supply all your greed (or even all your wants or desires); it
says He will provide all your need. Some people falsely
teach that all we need to do if we really want something
is to claim it in faith. This is often referred to as "Word/
faith" teaching, but it really is "lack of Word/presumption"
teaching. No, God is not some Santa in heaven, but a wise
and loving Heavenly Father who, in His infinite wisdom,
may choose to say no to some of our requests for our own
good.

I am thankful that God overrules some of our prayers.
As Proverbs 30:8–9 says, "Give me neither poverty nor
riches! Give me just enough to satisfy my needs. For if
I grow rich, I may deny you and say, 'Who is the Lord?'
And if I am too poor, I may steal and thus insult God's
holy name" (NIV).

Imagine what would happen if you were to give a child
absolutely everything that he or she wanted. What would
happen is that you would raise a spoiled, undisciplined,
hyperactive monster. This can apply to our relationship with God as well. He knows what is good for us. He
knows what we need. And He knows what we don't need.

The Secret of Contentment

So don't be afraid to give. I'm not just speaking of
finances. I am speaking of giving in general. Jesus said,
"It is more blessed to give than to receive" (Acts 20:35).

Haven't you found that principle to be true in your life? Have you discovered the joy of giving? This is the secret of contentment.

You can go through life asking, "What about my needs?" or you can say, "God has really blessed me. He has provided for me. I had a meal this morning. I have clothes on my back. I have a roof over my head. Now what can I do for someone else?"

You can apply this attitude to marriage as well. In a marriage where there is constant friction, it is usually because two people went into the relationship each saying, "What can you do for me?" But why not go into it God's way and esteem the other person above yourself? When you have two people going into a marriage asking, "How can I fulfill this person? What can I do to bless this person? What can I do to meet this person's needs?", that will be a blessed marriage.

When you start thinking of others instead of yourself, one day you will wake up and discover that you are a happy person. But it won't be because you have chased after the things you thought would fulfill you. You will find you are a happy person because you have your priorities in order.

Are you content right now? Or are you thinking, *I am almost content ... If I could just get this promotion ... If I could just upgrade my computer ... If I had a little more horsepower in my vehicle ... If my house were just a little bit bigger.*

If that is the case, then you are missing the point. It is always beyond your reach —and always will be. You need to have a relationship with God so that your contentment doesn't come from what you have, but from whom you know.

You can find contentment today. If you choose to do things God's way, you will be able to say, like David, "The Lord is my shepherd; I shall not want."

Afterword: The Joy of Knowing God

Maybe you are facing some type of crisis right now ... troubles at home ... troubles with the kids ... troubles with your husband or wife ... troubles with the in-laws ... troubles at work ... physical troubles ... aches and pains and problems that the doctors can't cure.

Or maybe things are going reasonably well. In fact, they are going so well that you can't figure out why you are so miserable. Everything is OK in your life for the most part, yet there is an emptiness inside you. You are not a happy person.

Maybe you have chased after possessions or success in your career in an attempt to find happiness. Maybe you have tried to fill a void with sexual relationships. Maybe you have turned to alcohol or drugs.

Jesus will change you and give you a whole new outlook on life. He will give you joy in the place of sorrow and fulfillment in the place of emptiness. He will give you purpose in the place of aimlessness. Best of all, He will give you heaven in the place of hell—if you will come to Him.

So how do you do that? First of all, you admit that you are a sinner. You come to God sorry for your sin and willing to turn from it and put your complete faith in Jesus Christ as your Savior and Lord. Then He will pardon you and forgive you of every sin you have ever committed.

He will make you a Christian. Then you can start experiencing the promises of joy you have been reading about in this book.

Have you done this? Have you asked Christ to come into your life? Do you know for certain right now that your sin is forgiven? If not, would you like to? I want to give you an opportunity to do this today. Below is a simple prayer. By praying this prayer and meaning it in your heart, you can make a commitment or a recommitment to Jesus Christ:

> Dear Lord Jesus, I know I am a sinner. I believe You died for my sins. Right now, I turn from my sins and open the door of my heart and life. I confess You as my personal Lord and Savior. Thank you for saving me. Amen.

The Bible tells us, "If we confess our sins, He is faithful and just to forgive us our sins and cleanse us from all unrighteousness" (1 John 1:9). If you just prayed that prayer and meant it, then Jesus Christ has now taken residence in your heart! Your decision to follow Christ means God has forgiven you and that you will spend eternity in heaven. It means you will be ready to meet Christ when He returns.

To help you grow in your newfound faith, be sure to make the following a part of your life each day: read the Bible regularly, pray, spend time with other Christians by going to church, and tell others about your faith in Christ.

For additional resources to help you learn more about what it means to know God and to be a follower of Jesus Christ, please visit http://www.harvest.org/knowgod/.

Notes

1. C. S. Lewis, *Mere Christianity,* revised ed. (San Francisco: HarperCollins Publishers, 2001), 50.

2. Orla Healy, "Magazine Vows to Continue JFK Jnr's Work, by George," *Independent.i.e.*, August 29, 1999; http://www. independent.ie/world-news/magazine-vows-to-continue-jfk-jnrs-work-by-george-520408.html.

3. "Are We Happy Yet?" *PewResearchCenter Publications,* February 13, 2006; http://pewresearch.org/pubs/301/are-we-happy-yet/.

4. "Jesus Christ's Effect on History," *Why-Jesus.com*; http://www. why-jesus.com/history.htm.

5. John Stuart Mill, *Nature, the Utility of Religion, and Theism,* 2nd ed. (London: Longmans, Green, Reader, and Dyer, 1874), 254.

6. "Jesus Christ's Effect on the Minds of the Greatest Intellects," *Why-the-Bible.com*; http://www.why-the-bible.com/intellect.htm.

7. Lewis, *Mere Christianity*, 52.

8. Leonard Sweet, quoted by William B. Oden in "Part of a Sermon I Will Never Forget," *North Texas United Methodist Reporter,* February 5, 1999.

About the Author

Greg Laurie is the pastor of Harvest Christian Fellowship (one of America's largest churches) in Riverside, California. He is the author of over thirty books, including the Gold Medallion Award winner, *The Upside-Down Church*, as well as *Every Day with Jesus; Are We Living in the Last Days?*; *Marriage Connections; Losers and Winners, Saints and Sinners;* and his new biography, *Lost Boy.* You can find his study notes in the *New Believer's Bible* and the *Seeker's Bible.* Host of the nationally syndicated radio program, *A New Beginning,* Greg Laurie is also the founder and featured speaker for Harvest Crusades—contemporary, large-scale evangelistic out-reaches, which local churches organize nationally and internationally.

He and his wife, Cathe, live in Southern California.

Other AllenDavid books Published by Kerygma Publishing

Visit:

www.kerygmapublishing.com
www.allendavidbooks.com
www.harvest.org